MY TIME

MY TIME

Thousands went to Broadway—Millions went to Auschwitz

Jack Edgerton
Member of the WRITERS GROUP

11/5/06

Liz —
I wish all the best for you in life. May you always be happy.
Love —
Uncle Jack

iUniverse, Inc.
New York Lincoln Shanghai

MY TIME
Thousands went to Broadway—Millions went to Auschwitz

Copyright © 2006 by Jack Edgerton

All rights reserved. No part of this book may be used or reproduced by any means, graphic, electronic, or mechanical, including photocopying, recording, taping or by any information storage retrieval system without the written permission of the publisher except in the case of brief quotations embodied in critical articles and reviews.

iUniverse books may be ordered through booksellers or by contacting:

iUniverse
2021 Pine Lake Road, Suite 100
Lincoln, NE 68512
www.iuniverse.com
1-800-Authors (1-800-288-4677)

ISBN-13: 978-0-595-39355-8 (pbk)
ISBN-13: 978-0-595-85005-1 (cloth)
ISBN-13: 978-0-595-83751-9 (ebk)
ISBN-10: 0-595-39355-1 (pbk)
ISBN-10: 0-595-85005-7 (cloth)
ISBN-10: 0-595-83751-4 (ebk)

Printed in the United States of America

#TXu-159-924
Content and front jacket artwork
United States Copyright Office—Library of Congress
All Rights Reserved

By Jack Edgerton

Front jacket slogan:
"Consider if this is a woman without hair and without a name with no more strength to remember, her eyes empty and her womb cold. She dies because of a yes or a no."

(Primo Levi)

To **Natalie, Jasmin, Laurin, Sarah, Cole, and Sabrina** with all my love—Grandpa

To **Mrs. Sawyer,** my creative writing teacher at OCC, wherever you are, I want to thank you for your inspiration many, many years ago. "History is written by the victors, so do your research well."

Thanks **Michelle** for all of your computer help and proofreading.

Contents

PREFACE xiii

Part I	**MEMORIES**
CHAPTER 1	WHO WAS ON THE ROOF? 3
CHAPTER 2	CHESSIE 6
CHAPTER 3	K—3 8
CHAPTER 4	ST. MARY'S ACADEMY a.k.a. CATHEDRAL . . . 10
CHAPTER 5	LEVY 13
CHAPTER 6	THE NEIGHBORHOOD 15
CHAPTER 7	STREET TRAFFIC 17
CHAPTER 8	WORKING FOR RINGLING 19
CHAPTER 9	AMUSEMENTS 21
CHAPTER 10	GRANDMA BURNS 24
CHAPTER 11	THE HOMESTEAD 26
CHAPTER 12	WATER 29
CHAPTER 13	CADET LIFE 33
CHAPTER 14	MY LIFE FOR THE NEXT FIVE YEARS 38
CHAPTER 15	OUT FOR A STROLL 41
CHAPTER 16	EUROPE 44

CHAPTER 17	DOWN SOUTH	47
CHAPTER 18	1961	49
CHAPTER 19	COLLEGE LIFE	51
CHAPTER 20	JOE BURNS' LEGACY	53
CHAPTER 21	CONFRONTATIONS	56
CHAPTER 22	BEING A DAD	63
CHAPTER 23	BUSINESS BENEFITS	67
CHAPTER 24	RAG DOLL	72
CHAPTER 25	DIB	78
CHAPTER 26	HAVING FUN	80
CHAPTER 27	STRANGE HAPPENINGS	86
CHAPTER 28	MOM	89
CHAPTER 29	TWIN TERROR—MURDER IN THE MORNING	93
Part II	**EVERTHING IS "SWELL" 1943**	
CHAPTER 30	THE HOMEFRONT	99
CHAPTER 31	LOCAL BOYS	103
CHAPTER 32	"HERE'S LOOKING AT YOU KID"	108
CHAPTER 33	"ROCK AND ROLL IS HERE TO STAY"	110
CHAPTER 34	"THE GREAT WHITE WAY"	111
Part III	**DEMONS UNLEASHED**	
CHAPTER 35	A NEW BOARD GAME	117
CHAPTER 36	EUROPE BECOMES A GRAVEYARD	120
CHAPTER 37	OSWIECIM a.k.a. AUSCHWITZ	123
CHAPTER 38	DIDN'T KNOW OR DIDN'T CARE	129
CHAPTER 39	TWO JEWS	131

CHAPTER 40	WHEN FREE WILL IS SURPRESSED, THE SPIRIT IS TAKEN AWAY	135
CHAPTER 41	POLES, JEWS, and LAKOTA	137
CHAPTER 42	IT CONTINUES	140
CHAPTER 43	TAKE A NUMBER	144
CHAPTER 44	ENTER ON A TRAIN—EXIT UP THE CHIMNEY	147
CHAPTER 45	SUFFER THE CHILDREN	148
CHAPTER 46	BEAUTIFUL COUNTRY UGLY MEMORIES	150
CHAPTER 47	FIRST HAND KNOWLEDGE	152
CHAPTER 48	I.G. FARBEN at AUSCHWITZ—MONOWITZ—BUNA	157
CHAPTER 49	HENRY "HEINRICH" FORD	166
CHAPTER 50	WRAP UP	169

APPENDIX for 1943 175
BIBLIOGRAPHY 183
ABOUT THE AUTHOR 193

PREFACE

    Last Spring I was thinking that I had better write something down about my life so that my children, grandchildren, or anyone else for that matter, could read how it was to grow up in *MY TIME*. Should I ever have Alzheimer's, someone can read this book to me about someone I once knew—ME! Who knows, maybe I'll have memory connections. This will also serve as a means of communication to my family after I'm gone.

    How little I knew about the life of my grandparents. Both of my grandfathers died before I was born. At their graveside on Memorial Day, I was reflecting on the limited knowledge I have of Grandpa Burns and the embarrassment of knowing absolutely nothing about Grandpa Edgerton. I never recalled my dad talking about his father. I guess I should have shown more interest by asking questions.

    What were their lives like? What were their hopes and desires for their children? I'm sure times were different then, as they were while I was growing up. I would like to attempt to tell you how it was to grow up in *MY TIME*. This is not to presume that all guys and gals my approximate age had the same experiences along this journey. It is just my opportunity to let you know my observations, my slant on life. I have a tendency to color outside of the lines—no rose-colored glasses for me! These are the stories of my childhood, of young adulthood, as a married man, father, and grandfather.

    Autobiographical happenings can tend to be exaggerated, but I'll try to stick to the facts as best I can remember them. Use your imagination on the journey and try to experience what it was like back then. We're going to explore my neighborhood, my city, my country, and other places as well. I'm going to paint a picture for you, but with words.

    I have met, and continue to meet, some very interesting people—some famous, some just day-to-day folks but every bit as important, nonetheless. I have been very fortunate to have traveled all over the world so it has given me the opportunity to experience different cultures and viewpoints.

I look at life as a story; major chapters developing as we move along. I look at each day as turning a page. So, want to come on a trip with me? You might get angry, you might laugh, you might cry. But hey, that's what life is like. So cuddle up in your easy chair, open up your mind to possible new ideas and thoughts. Come reminisce with me or learn for the very first time.

Although the first part of my story is autobiographical, it is none the less, historical. Many experiences of mine would be non-existent today.

Parts of the story are humorous, some are educational, others, are terrifying.

I
MEMORIES

Time travel to the past is a…memory.

1

WHO WAS ON THE ROOF?

All afternoon I found myself going back and forth between the kitchen and the living room. Mom is baking cookies and she has me using tin cookie cutters to cut out shapes of Christmas trees, Santa with bags over his shoulder, candy canes, wreaths made of holly, angels, and the like. You remember-you probably did the same. In the living room I'm "helping" my sister string popcorn and cranberries on thread with a needle. They will go on the tree later in the day with all the other ornaments. These are a couple of projects, Mom has, to keep me busy and out of her way so she can concentrate on dinner and homemade baked goods for the neighbors, or for whoever drops in to visit.

My dad had a nickname. My sister called him "*Dib*" so that's who he is in this narrative. Dib is at work and should be home soon. What could be keeping him so long? I want everything to move faster so that tomorrow arrives quicker.

I'm very tempted to try some ribbon candy or hard candies that are in a colorful dish but I've been warned not to eat any until after dinner. There are also dried dates, apricots, and other fruits on display but at my age they don't look appetizing, same thing for fruitcake.

Dib has come home a little early so we can eat and get going on the tree decorating. We got the tree the other day at Scornick's gas station after much scrutinizing over height and shape and price.

Down from the attic he brings box after box of decorations that have been handed down over the generations. There are several that I'm not allowed to touch because Aunt Bertha gave them to us a long time ago and they had been on great-grandma's tree in Denver. Victorian ornaments are so colorful and unique but at the same time, very fragile. Many will be broken over the years as they drop off the branches when the tree dries and the needles fall off. Also, we had a cat that would knock them off and play with them. The ones left today are in my sister Joan's care.

Dib brought the tree in through the front door as it's closest to the living room and Mom doesn't want needles all through the house. It's one of the rare times that door is open. We always seem to use the kitchen door at the side of the house. Perhaps over the years, like evolution, builders will phase out front doors as being useless.

The first items to go on the tree are the bubble lights. For those of you not familiar with them, they replaced actual candles that were used years ago but were dangerous because they started fires and many a home was destroyed this way. Anyhow, after you arranged them on the tree, either my sister or I got to turn them on. After a few minutes they would warm up and start to bubble. The glass tubes contained a colored liquid that provided lots of festivity to the tree. Added to this were the ornaments, the tinsel, and, of course, the popcorn and cranberries.

Now for the stockings hung on the mantel, some milk and cookies for Santa, a carrot for the reindeer and we should be all set. My dad and sister are doing something together across the room while I'm in Mom's lap. She is reading a story to me titled *"The Night Before Christmas."* It was written by Clement Clarke Moore with pictures by Thomas Nast. He wrote it on Christmas Eve in 1822 as a gift for his children. For me this was bliss and peace all wrapped up in one. Little did I know what was going on in the rest of the world. We'll talk about that later.

Up to bed I go, but Joan can stay up later because she's four years older. As I just get tucked in, a horrible thought comes to me and I rush down the stairs in tears. You see Dib had built a fire in the fireplace so he and Mom could relax and enjoy some eggnog. Wrong! Anyone can tell you that Santa comes down the chimney. Mom just read that to me. There can't be a fire or Santa will get burned and he'll leave and we won't get toys. So, needless to say, I wouldn't go back to bed until Dib put out the fire. I wasn't too popular.

In the morning everything is magical. How did all of this stuff fit into Santa's sleigh and how did it get down such a small chimney? That's the inquisitive side of me starting up, I guess. I let everyone know that I knew he came because I heard him on the roof last night. My bedroom was on the top floor so it was easy for me to hear him and his reindeer moving around up there. You have to pretend you're sleeping because *"he knows if you're awake."*

I had an orange in my stocking so I knew that I was good. Oranges were for good girls and boys while coal was for bad. My wife to this day gets coal in hers because she's *"naughty and nice!"* Presents from Mom and Dad were generally under the tree and presents from Santa were by the fireplace.

Under the tree for me is a wind-up, tin train that goes on a track around the tree (drives the cat crazy), **Tinker Toys, Lincoln Logs,** brightly colored blocks to get you started learning your alphabet, numbers, and colors, and a puzzle of the U.S. In my stocking were socks, comic books, a jar of peanuts or a box of **Cracker Jacks**, a roll of **Life Savers**, a book about Dick, Jane, Spot, and Puff, some candy, a gingerbread man, a candy cane and most importantly—an orange!

The wind-up train was later replaced by a **Lionel** set which had track, a transformer that could control two trains at the same time, **Plasticville** buildings, little cars, trucks, people, and trees for landscaping. This has recently been passed on to my grandson, Cole, to take care of.

The set was purchased by my parents from the E.W. Edwards Department Store in Syracuse for the price of $29.00. There was a train show held here in Syracuse recently and the engine alone was appraised at $5,000 to $6,000, what a nice value increase. How I used to love to look down the track and see the train coming toward my face with the light on and the smoke puffing out of the stack. It was really special with the lights off in the room.

Years later while walking home from school, I noticed that some homes didn't have a chimney and Dib explained that Santa probably came in their front door with their presents. I guess we had better not phase out those front doors, after all.

Our neighborhood, I would say, was made up of predominantly Jewish families. The old "Jew Town" had been demolished for urban renewal and the displaced families had moved up to our neighborhood. My Jewish friends told me that they didn't celebrate Christmas and they didn't have a Christmas tree. Some said they had a Hanukkah bush if both parents weren't Jewish. How did Santa know which houses to go to? Well that's one of my earliest memories. I'll tell you about another as our journey moves down the track.

2

CHESSIE

When you get a chance, pick up a book titled *Chessie*. I don't remember the author's name but I'm sure you can get it at your local library. As I recall, *Chessie* is about a kitten that rides on the Chesapeake and Ohio Railroad and all the fun and mischief she gets into.

Grandma lives next door to us and is coming up to watch my younger brother, Bill, while Joan and I along with Mom and Dib are headed downtown to the train station in Syracuse. You see, we are going to take the New York Central train to Denver to see Aunt Bertha and my great-grandma, Lillian.

Mom had bought the book to read to me along the way to make it more of an adventure. By identifying with the characters in the book, it would make the trip more interesting for me. It worked! We had a Pullman car and porters just like the pictures in the book showed. This was going to be fun! The trip to Denver went by fairly quickly as I can remember as a four year old.

We were met at the train station and brought to my aunt's house. I remember a long street with large, beautiful houses on it. My aunt had a wire-haired terrier named Whirligig who promptly spotted us getting out of the car and made a dash down the walkway to what I thought was a greeting. My sister bent over to pet the dog and immediately was a bloody mess. Whirligig had jumped up to her face and latched on to her lower lip and wouldn't let go until my dad's shoe came in contact with the dog's side. A rush to the hospital was next—so much for that day.

We all went to a natural history museum the next day where I got my first exposure to dinosaur skeletons. That place was really neat! We also went up in the mountains to see their cabin in the Rockies. I don't recall the train ride back home at all.

One other early memory was riding on the very last trolley in the city. My dad found out that the last trip of the last route would be near our house. My mom drove us downtown to get on the trolley headed to Croly Street. Dib said to try and remember the ride because we were making history as the very last riders. She was there to meet us at the end of the line and we watched as it turned around and went back to the trolley barn, empty. Some of these old trolleys were converted to small diners, others ended up in the junkyard. The overhead wires were taken down and the tracks were either torn up and removed or paved over. Gasoline or diesel powered buses were making their entrance.

3
K—3

Kindergarten through third grade at Charles Andrews School was fairly uneventful. I remember having really nice teachers and enjoying school. Playing marbles at recess time was a favorite activity. There were "cat's eyes," "steelies" (ball bearings), and marbles made out of hard brown clay. The rules of play seemed to change every week but if you ended up with a drawstring bag of "steelies," you were the tops. There seemed to be a lot of these in circulation. It might have had something to do with Rollway Bearing, now Killian Bearing, being located in Syracuse. They made ball bearings for the war effort.

Up the street from our school was the Elmcrest Children's Center. It was a facility for children from "broken" homes or for troubled kids that were unmanageable at home. They usually kept to themselves at recess time unless Wanda, a pretty Native American girl, decided to go on the warpath with her friends. They would come charging down the hill like Comanches attacking a wagon train, thereby scattering the rest of us. They must have watched the same Westerns as I did.

Every day at lunchtime we all walked home-no school buses back then (you've heard that before, I'm sure). It was probably four to five blocks each way with thirty to thirty-five minutes to eat. I looked forward to lunch as Mom always tried to get us to try different foods, but I would say that PB&J was still our favorite. Soap operas were on in the middle of the day. These shows were actually sponsored by companies promoting laundry products such as **Ajax, Tide, Duz,** and others.

Ann was a pretty little blonde who happened to be in third grade with me. Now most every boy at that age has no interest in girls. I guess I wasn't normal because it bothered me that she was moving away never to be seen again. I just had to come up with a little present of some sort to let her know that she'd be missed.

My mom had purchased a small, inexpensive tea set for me to give to her. All little girls played with dolls and this would remind her of me. Pretty good logic for an eight-year old, don't you think?

4

ST. MARY'S ACADEMY a.k.a. CATHEDRAL

For some reason, and I've never been told why, my sister and I started attending a Catholic school downtown. The Cathedral School was run by the Sisters of Charity. My next three years were spent learning next to nothing and putting up with nuns for the duration. Unless you've gone to a Catholic school you probably can't either empathize or sympathize with me.

Joan and I were to take a city bus downtown everyday and for her that meant without me tagging along. She would either eat breakfast earlier or do without just so her younger brother wasn't at the bus stop with her. She didn't realize how stressful it was for me as a young kid to be alone in the city in 4th grade. I'd prevail though, and more often as not I was there when the bus pulled up—probably payback for the hours of listening to her practice her accordion lessons or the endless hours of various country western singers such as Eddie Arnold on her record player. Must be the reason that I can't stand C-W today!

Sister Dominica was our teacher for 4th grade. She was a sweet little old lady who quite often fell asleep at her desk. Besides the fact that she was nearly deaf, you can guess that 4th grade was not too challenging. A 180 degree change was Sister Mary Catherine for 5th grade. All the kids feared her but I hit it off with her right away and had no problems for the year and I thought that she was a fairly good teacher.

I did, however, make two close friends—one was Dwayne Jackson and the other George Lundy. One was black, the other Puerto Rican. If I ever spent my carfare or lost it, I had to walk, and that meant not through the nicest of neighborhoods. They were there for me. Usually 7 to 8 blocks of walking with them and I was safe on my own for the rest of the way.

It was my first exposure to prejudice—not from them, but unfortunately from my dad, of all people. I invited them to our house to play after school one day and it turned out to be the only day.

My mom made us snacks and lemonade, my dad made them go home. I was very mad and later had a long talk with my mom. She wasn't brought up that way and she couldn't understand his ignorance.

I lost a lot of respect for Dib on that day. I guess I started seeing him in a different, confusing light. It was as if I was viewing him through crackled glass—the light comes through, but the image isn't clear.

I had a nun in sixth grade, Sister Florence from Hell. She would come out of the convent next door after she had her gruel for lunch, with her arms crossed and that superior glare which made the kids get off the sidewalk like, "the parting of the Red Sea." The first seven months she was the ruler of her domain and the last three, very meek. You see, she ran into my dad's temper!

She told me to stay after school one day for no apparent reason. It was not a discipline issue, she just selected kids to stay after and do HER chores. To make a long story short, I was told in a rather harsh tone to close all of the windows in the classroom. I could barely reach them without being on tiptoes. This one particular window came slamming down with all my body weight on it not realizing that there was a large fish bowl under it that nobody had moved out of the way. Glass, water, fish, and pebbles went flying all over the room!

She was out of her chair in a rage coming at me. She grabbed my arms and was shaking me until screams from classmates caught her attention. Her pearly white, starched bib was all splattered with blood. A chunk of glass had sliced through the artery of my arm just below my wrist.

With every beat of my heart, fresh blood was spraying everywhere. She had the sense to know that her cords around her waist could be used for something other than hitting us. A sort of tourniquet was made to halt the bleeding until my dad could get there from his office to take me to the doctor's for stitches.

The next day, there was a heated discussion between my dad, the nun, and the principal. I really could do no wrong for the rest of the semester.

There was one day that I was reading by the window when I happened to look across the street at the **Greyhound Bus** terminal. There was a man standing on the second floor ledge. He dove as if he was going into a swimming pool but instead his head hit the parking meter below.

Whenever we heard a siren, the nuns would tell us to kneel down and silently say a prayer. I told this same nun that we had all better kneel down and say a prayer for the guy. And from her desk she questioned me that how could I possibly know that he was dead! "Well Sister," I said, "his brains are all over the sidewalk." That was my first, but not only exposure to suicide.

Add to this the fact that the Onondaga County Morgue was visible out the other window, and that we constantly saw a parade of dead bodies, I had enough! Classmates would call out, "the meat wagon is here again!"—so much for Catholic school.

5

LEVY

I'm back at public school for seventh grade. For me, and my neighborhood friends, it means attending the worst and roughest that Syracuse had to offer at the time. You can talk all you want about gangs today but they were just as bad back then, if not more so. We learned to walk or ride our bikes in a large group just to get to school and back home in one piece. I'm not exaggerating!

You probably wonder, what could possibly happen in seventh grade? Trouble didn't originate from kids my age but from older kids who were held back, sometimes several times, because of poor grades or because they were troublemakers. They were called "dukes" and wore "DA" haircuts smothered with a gel called **Pomade**. That's the way it was then.

These kids, for the most part, were poor white from the "housing project" now called Rolling Green Estates. The name couldn't be farther from the truth. There's nothing green—all tarvia and it doesn't resemble an estate in the least. Those buildings today are the residence for black families. There was a volatile mix at this school—poor whites, wealthy whites, Catholics, Jews, Protestants, a few Asian families all thrown in together—sort of what the movie called a *"blackboard jungle"*.

During this one year, an English teacher was grabbed in a hallway and pulled into a boy's bathroom where she was raped. Nobody knew who did it or if they did know they weren't going to "rat."

Mr. LaVoy was our shop teacher and you probably couldn't have asked for a nicer guy. Our official project was to make a wooden tray for silverware to eventually bring home for our moms. On this particular day, a group of six or seven guys were over on the other side of the shop class where he discovered them making "zip" guns. A fight ensued whereas he was beat to a bloody mess with lumber that the boys had picked up from the floor. They hit him repeatedly over the head. He was rushed to the hospital, and to my knowledge, did not return to our school.

Car radios, back then, gained reception through an outside antenna. These were snapped off where they attached to the fender as they were used as barrels for these .22 caliber "zip" guns-relatively simple to make and very deadly at close range.

Let me break here before I continue with education issues. I'd like to do some reminiscing with you.

6

THE NEIGHBORHOOD

Ridgeway Avenue is situated on the eastside of Syracuse—a few blocks east of the "housing project" and a few blocks west of Lemoyne College. Our house sat on top of the hill that is above Erie Blvd., formerly the Erie Canal. It was a very rural street at one point in time consisting of my grandfather's orchard and berry bushes on one side of the lane and Judge Hickock's house and property on the other. Over the years, several lots were sold off to people for building houses.

My grandparents lived down at the corner and our house was on the hill next door to them. They had replaced their large Victorian farmhouse with a Florida-style ranch. The chickens, ducks, and other animals were pretty much gone by the time I was born. The chicken coop was converted into a clubhouse for the four of us and our friends. We could use it year-round because it had a wood-burning stove inside. We called it, "the shed."

What a view we had from up there! You could see the entire skyline of Syracuse as you looked to the west. To the north you could look over towards Eastwood or look down in the valley and watch the trains go by. It was pleasant growing up on Ridgeway. We had nice neighbors, for the most part. There were approximately three acres of land to run around on, not to mention the huge woods behind us that must have been another forty acres or more. It was a great place to go exploring, climb trees and build tree forts. In the woods was a deep ravine we called the "gully." In the lower part was a fenced area where the muck farmers kept their horses. Every once in awhile we'd go on a round-up chasing the horses and quite often they'd chase us.

Muck is that black, nutrient-rich, bottomland very suitable for growing celery, onions, and lettuce.

I had a large number of friends as did my sisters and brother. Our house was often the focal point for gatherings. We had a pool table in the basement and the first television set on our street. I remember our first program was *The Lone Ranger* on a Thursday night at 7:00pm. I went around behind the television to see where the picture was coming from but my dad told me that the picture came in through the antenna. Interesting how a horse and rider could go through a wire into a box!

As I previously mentioned, our neighborhood was comprised of predominately Jewish families. As synagogues were relocated, they moved in an easterly direction from an area in the city called "Jew Town." There were also Polish, Irish, and Italians in the same area—lots of different cultures, for the most part, all getting along—not so in Europe, as I would find out later.

7

STREET TRAFFIC

    Let's look at things that went by in front of our house, maybe yours also. I can still remember the clomp-clomp-clomp of the horse coming up the hill pulling the milk wagon. We really looked forward to this on a hot day because the milkman would give us chips of ice to suck on. You see, the wagon was not refrigerated. The milk, eggs, cheese, and butter were kept cold by blocks of ice packed in straw. The reins to the horse were always limp. That horse knew the route by heart and knew every stop. The milkman had a metal carrier to bring the products to our milk box which was a passageway approx. 15"x15" into our kitchen so that the dairy products wouldn't spoil outside in the heat. There was a door on the outside and one on the inside. It often was a life saver to get into the house if you forgot your key. A child could crawl through as I did many a time.

    Just about every week you could hear a man calling out in broken English that he had fresh produce. Vegetables were on one side of this cart and fruit was displayed on the other. This too was horse drawn but his horse was not as smart as the milkman's. He probably didn't understand Italian! Quite often he had fresh chickens for sale that he would pull out of a cage. He had a watering can with him so that he could spray the fruits and vegetables to make them look fresh but he couldn't fool my mom.

    Another Italian was the knife grinder. He carried this heavy wooden frame over his back, which had a grinding wheel, a foot pedal, and an attached seat. He would walk down the sidewalk ringing a bell that he carried in one hand. He usually didn't get much work from us because we were in the knife business and always had sharp ones in the drawer. My mom felt sorry for him though, and would try to find something for him to do even if we really didn't need it. She would always offer him a glass of water or lemonade to help him get through the day.

As kids we always became excited when the police would go by on their motorcycles. Some had sidecars to carry an extra policeman. We had one who lived up the street from us who would often bring his friends home for lunch. That was a big treat having five or six ride up the hill together. Boy, were they loud! We'd ride our bikes up to his house hoping that we could get a ride in that sidecar—it never happened. He died a few years later chasing a speeder. His tires slid on gravel as he was turning a corner and his motorcycle slammed into a tree.

We also had an ice cream man. For years he had to pedal a large, white, insulated box on a bicycle frame before they became motorized. Once the **Skippy** ice cream man had a truck, you could always tell when it was time for dinner—that's when he showed up!

One other fellow, who came once, had a horse and a camera with a tripod. Cowboy movies were big then and most kids had some kind of cowboy outfit with cap guns. This fellow was capitalizing on that by bringing a real horse to your house and you could get your picture taken as well—for a price.

People that came to our door were usually the **Fuller Brush** man, a man selling **Stanley Home Products**, a **Hoover** vacuum cleaner demonstrator, or an occasional insurance salesman telling us you could get insurance for pennies a day. Later I remember my mom being bothered by men pushing aluminum siding or driveway sealing. I guess you would now call it door-to-door spam. I wish that someone back then mowed lawns, then I wouldn't have to. Three acres was a lot of grass!

Homes up the street had coal deliveries in the fall just before the cold weather came. It was kind of neat to watch them hook up the chutes that would go through the casement window into the coal bin in the basement. We never had coal delivery as we were the first to get natural gas. Most homes converted in no time because it was a cleaner fuel source. The advantage of having coal meant that you had ashes to carry in your car trunk in case you got stuck in the snow.

8

WORKING FOR RINGLING

A special treat was when the circus came to town. It was either, *The Ringling Brothers, Barnum & Bailey Circus* or *Cole Brothers-Clyde Beatty Circus* which would stop off in Syracuse for a few days. Generally, the trains would pull into the New York Central freight yards downtown. We would beg our dad to go and watch them unload. There were usually two trains-one for the animals and tent equipment-the other for the performers and their gear. They would unload early in the morning, as effortlessly as they had done hundreds of times before. Each person seemed to know his job from so much repetition. Elephants were used to push the wagons off the trains.

They would form-up on Erie Blvd. and then parade down Salina Street to a destination just out of town in the valley where they were to set up for the show. The smell, the sights, and the sounds, were different from anything I ever experienced before. I had seen wild animals but only at our small zoo.

Many years later my brother and I worked one day for *Ringling* in Auburn, NY. They were on a farewell tour of the Big Top. The outdoor show became a thing of the past. They were moving indoors to places such as Madison Square Garden. Consequently, if your town did not have a sizeable indoor arena, they wouldn't appear.

We worked all day throwing tent stakes off the wagon where some were pounded into the ground by hand or most generally by steam hammers. For this, we had lunch with the crew and the clowns and we received six free tickets for the evening performance. It was neat to see the performers in their acts and to know that we sat with these same people at lunchtime. I wouldn't trade that for anything!

It was my first exposure to people that most people felt were not normal and were treated as "freaks." Due to a birth defect that affected their appearance or that they were born as dwarfs or midgets, the public looked down on them. I suppose the circus was a good place to hide. Putting on a mask or makeup enabled them to "fit-in." They were in a company of friends with similar situations.

The circus seems to come here possibly once a year under the name of *The Tigris Shrine Circus*. It's here for a few days, but it's not the same for me. Maybe if I were still a child I'd be in awe but I'm looking now through adult eyes. I guess I'm too much of an "old fart." That's what my daughters call me, so I might as well use the term.

9

AMUSEMENTS

Besides the circus we had lots of other things to do including the Saturday matinees at the Westcott Theatre. You could spend the afternoon there for $1.00. Two feature movies and one half hour of cartoons would cost fifty cents. The rest was spent on popcorn, candy, and a soft drink. Cowboys like Gene Autry, Roy Rogers, Hoot Gibson, Tom Mix, Lash Larue, John Wayne, Bob Steele, and Hop-A-Long Cassidy, brought the Wild West to your seat and imagination into your being. The plots were usually the same but it was the adventure we were after.

I further enjoyed *"The Bowery Boys"* with Leo Gorcey and Huntz Hall. These types of movies were soon replaced by gangster, science fiction and scary movies. I remember being terrified by *"THEM"* and *"THE CREATURE FROM THE BLACK LAGOON."* Today's kids would probably laugh at this entertainment. Outer space would visit the movies with flying saucers and creatures from Mars.

We would spend endless hours climbing trees, going to the park to go on the slide, teeter-totter, and some contraption that spun you around in circles that got you so dizzy that you couldn't stand up or walk straight. There were outside games played in the yard with names such as "Tom-Tom Pull-away", "Red Rover-Red Rover", and "Duck-Duck Goose" We would ride bikes by the hour and cover mile after mile. Remember attaching playing cards with clothes-pins to make the sound of a motor? It gave you such freedom and your parents had no idea where you were.

We'd go to Botnik's Drug Store where they could mix wonderful drinks and ice cream sodas for very little money and you could hang out by the hour talking. On a dare I took a pack of gum without paying for it and when my dad found out, I had to go back and pay with an apology to Mr. Botnik. Later, I felt funny about going there again.

You have to remember that these were the days before television and way before i-pods, computers, and *MTV*. Life was simple then. You could amuse yourself by the hour with an **Erector Set**. You could call up friends and have a sand-lot baseball or softball game, a touch football game, marbles, jacks, or just whittle a piece of wood with a pocket knife. In my dad's early years he was a carpenter so we had all kinds of tools to build things. He would help us with projects down in his shop in the basement after dinner or on weekends.

In the winter, of course, activities were different in Syracuse. We are known as the "snow capital of the country" where snow is measured each year in feet, not inches. It's called "lake effect" due to the fact that the cold air coming out of the northwest passes over Lake Ontario in the Great Lakes. The moisture evaporating off this lake is picked up by this wind, chilled, and dumped as snow in very high volume. So as a child you love it because of sliding, snow forts, skating, and "snow days"-meaning no school because the roads are impassable or the "wind chill" is too low. On days like this we could ride a sled down the hill to the bowling alley and hopefully you had someone older with you to keep score. Sliding had to be done before the plow came which usually spread ashes or salt on the road so the dads could get home from work.

It always seemed to my mom that no longer had she gotten us all dressed with snowsuit, boots, gloves or mittens, and a cap, then someone had to go to the bathroom and the whole process would start over again. We were always coming back to the house for dry socks, dry mittens, or hot cocoa. I can still today remember the stink of wool clothes drying on the register. You really slept well because of all the activity and fresh air. Do you remember clips on your snowsuit arms attached to your mittens so you wouldn't lose them and clothes pins with some sort of mark on them to keep your boots in pairs at school. For boys this was a nightmare, all boots or "galoshes" came in black. Try walking home with one boot and one shoe exposed.

Winter also meant ice skating at Beard Park in Fayetteville or, more often than not, a trip over to Drumlins Rink for the day. Speed skating was my forte. They also had a hockey rink and an area for figure skaters.

Amusements on the weekend might be a drive-in movie, a ride out in the country on back roads (the only way to travel according to my parents), or a trip to the local eatery in Dewitt called the Pig Stand for a hamburger, fries, and a malted shake. We might head downtown as there were no malls in our time. You went walking up and down Salina Street, "window shopping."

In smaller cities as ours, the days of the downtown department store are gone. They had multiple floors and an escalator or elevator to get you where you wanted to go. The elevator operator wore white gloves and would call out what was for sale on each floor. Floors had separate departments, hence the name. Quite often near the escalator was a floor person familiar with products in their area. Products were often demonstrated, as were our knives. This would attract a crowd similar to a "barker" at a state fair. Samples of food would be given away or you might get a spray of the latest perfume or cologne.

There were lots of movie theatres such as Loews Strand, Empire, R.K.O. Keith, Loews State, Eckel, Paramount, and the Bijou for downtown entertainment not to mention numerous neighborhood movie houses. My mother-in-law worked behind the candy counter at one of the theaters, so I was probably one of her best customers. There was quite a variety of movies at economical prices. I don't remember R or X pictures being shown or if movies were even rated back then.

It was a treat to go out to dinner at one of the great restaurants we had. Dining out was special. You had the opportunity to practice your manners out in public. My grandmother would quite often take me out to lunch to meet her friends. I wasn't a fussy eater—I was game for anything and I still am.

10

GRANDMA BURNS

My grandmother was born with the first name, Vita. If you're a student of Latin you'll know that the word vita means "life." Life is what she was all about. I remember her having spontaneous ice cream parties for the whole neighborhood. This gives you an idea of what great fun she was. She was a lover of animals and respected all of God's creatures. There were always dogs, cats, and canary birds at her house. One day I walked down to see her and I must have held the door open a little too long because one of her pet birds flew out the kitchen door and up into one of her trees. A canary will sing calling a mate, or if it's plain happy. That bird sang all day but he wouldn't come down. She learned from that episode to keep the birds in their cages.

The kitchen door was the entrance for somewhat-tamed squirrels. She would tap two walnuts together and they would come running to investigate. She'd leave the door open and go in the kitchen and sit still. She would tell me not to move or I would scare them. Little nuts and seeds had been placed on the floor for them to rob. I don't look at them today like she did. To me they are just rats with bushy tails!

Her husband, my grandfather, died the year before I was born. They had one child that lived. Fortunately, it was my mother or I wouldn't be here to write this. Four children from four different pregnancies just didn't make it.

They had money back then as my grandfather was an inventor and an astute businessman. They were able to take my mom on some nice trips (a love of which she passed on to us); and they had the finances to provide her with a four year degree in Fine Arts at Syracuse University. Prior to college she attended a private girl's school in Coral Gables, Florida. So I guess you could say they were "lace-curtain Irish".

Quite often, as I mentioned before, my grandmother would enjoy meeting her friends for lunch downtown. This one particular day she decided not to bring the dog. She was picking up a friend and the dog, a large German Shepard, made her friend nervous. The dog was put in the basement but it could see out the cellar window as the car went by. The dog tried to climb up some shelving to get out of the window. The shelves weren't attached to the wall and they fell over like dominoes. My grandfather's entire cut glass collection was on those shelves. When my grandmother arrived home later in the day she found the dog on the floor bleeding to death and all the glass broken.

My grandmother developed a condition called sugar diabetes, which would later take its toll on her. I remember her often telling me that she had to give herself a shot of medicine. She'd go in her bedroom and close the door so I wouldn't see. It prolonged her life but she eventually died in 1952.

The wake, as was the custom with the Irish then, was held at her house. I remember that the day before she was to be buried, my mom took us down to see her. She was the first person that I ever saw in a casket. She looked so peaceful but I was puzzled why she wasn't talking to me like she always did.

The hearse came the next morning to take her to church. We had a babysitter so we weren't able to say a final "good-bye." I loved my Grandma very much. I had another Grandma but she didn't live as close by. She lived in Marcellus for the last years of her life. Her name was "Granny" and she came here from Canada. I'll tell you about her heritage now.

11

THE HOMESTEAD

Dalkeith is a very small community in Glengary, tucked into the northeast corner of Ontario, Canada. It lies to the east of Ottawa and is about 5 miles west of the Quebec Province border. If you travel due north from Cornwall, which is on the St. Lawrence River, you're bound to run into it. Don't blink, or you'll miss it! This is where part of my roots is from. It was in this area that my dad, his parents, and siblings grew up before their exodus to the "states" when he was 7 or 8 years old. This makes me a first-generation American.

One summer when I was very young, I went on a trip up there with my dad, my sister, my cousin, and my aunt. The memory of this trip is so clear that it seems as though it happened yesterday—even though it was probably 50 years ago or more.

I felt as a child that it took forever to drive there. We took the old Route 11 before the days of the Interstate System developed by Eisenhower. We arrived in time for a chicken dinner with "all the fixin's" as they'd say. It was early to bed for me because I was invited to go to the creamery in the morning and that meant getting up at 5:00 A.M.! I was tired anyway from the long ride and sleeping in a down comforter was just the ticket for a good night sleep.

The trip to the creamery was not by car or truck but on a buckboard wagon drawn by horses. Wow, this was great! That milk wagon that came to our house was nothing compared to this. I first waited for Uncle Angus to come back from the barn before we had our breakfast. He was awake much earlier than I was because he had to milk the cows and give them hay and water. "You take care of the animals and they'll take care of you," he'd proclaim. Angus, by the way, was one of 13 children—8 boys and 5 girls—lots of help on that farm. I thought I had a lot of kids! Isabella MacMillan, my "Granny", was one of those girls.

Breakfast meant eggs, Canadian bacon, hot cornmeal Johnny cake with maple syrup, buckwheat pancakes, cornflakes with raw milk and honey, and a raspberry drink. Everything came from that farm except the cereal. I guess that's why breakfast is still my favorite meal of the day. Orange juice would have been a luxury. There was no morning paper or weather report. Being a farmer with years of experience, Angus could tell what weather was coming.

Now, out the door we go to climb up on the wagon. It's just the two of us- everyone else is still sleeping. Let them, I've got Uncle Angus to myself! The wagon had been loaded while I was picking up dishes in the kitchen.

We are going down an old country lane to the main road where we'll take a left turn to the creamery. On both sides of this lane is his property. There are sheep on one side, cows on the other. The bull is in the barn, the pigs in the sty, the chickens and geese wherever they want to roam. The horses are in front of us and they act like they're glad to be out of their stalls. He carries a gun with him in the wagon just in case we see a deer or a turkey. This augments their normal diet of farm-raised animals.

At the creamery we unloaded the raw milk, said our greetings, and bartered for cheese and other dairy products that Uncle Angus might need. No money was exchanged. On the way back he pretends to straighten the load in the back and hands me the reins. One horse looks back to see a young Yankee lad, still wet behind the ears, with this big grin on his face. I looked forward to this trip every day not to mention the breakfast. On this farm you were self-sufficient except for medicine and schooling.

There was a pond that was fed by a cold stream loaded with trout. When this froze over the ice was cut with big saws and dragged on a flat skid by the horses to an underground pit near the house where the ice was stacked between layers of straw or sawdust. Anything that had to be kept cold was placed down there since there was no refrigeration. When the pit was filled, boards were placed on top to form a roof and this was covered with sod for insulation. There was an entrance with steps where they would carry smoked hams, slabs of bacon, sides of beef, lamb, and pork, fruit, cheese, and vegetables for storage. The temperature in this underground room remained constant all year. You needed to wear a sweater if you were going to be down there for any length of time.

The "sugar bush" as they called it, was the woods nearby where the sugar maple trees grew. These were tapped in the spring when the sap was running.

The best flow was on warm days-cold nights. The sap was boiled in large vats in the sugar shack to produce syrup. It took many gallons of sap to produce one gallon of syrup. The shack was only used for syrup production so it would remain clean. In the front yard near the flower garden were the bee hives. Between the honey and the syrup you had sweeteners for the year.

All the meat except for wild game came from the farm. There was a huge vegetable garden and an orchard for fresh fruit. It sounds ideal, but a short growing season and harsh winters, made for a very tough existence. The house, by the way, was heated with firewood—no gas, coal, or oil in that region at that time. But, you know, that's what hardy, Scottish, families are accustomed to. That's their way of life up there—just like in the old country. The house is still there and I plan to visit the area this summer.

As a member of the Syracuse Scottish Pipe Band, I returned there many years later. Going to the Scottish Games in Maxville made me so proud of that side of my heritage. Maxville was the next town over, possibly 15 miles away. Three of my sons played with me in competition and in massed bands that day. If only Angus were alive to hear and see us, how proud he would have been. Just think, we could have stayed over for breakfast in the morning!

People always ask a piper what is worn under a kilt and I would always respond, "Nothing is worn, it's all in working condition!"

12

WATER

In my life, water seemed to play a very important part. Green Lakes State Park, Cazenovia Lake, Lake Placid, Skaneateles Lake, the North Atlantic, St. Lawrence River, Oswego River, Lake Ontario, and the ocean beaches of Florida, Hawaii, Paradise Island-Bahamas, Bermuda, Cancun, and Puerto Rico were all places that I visited or spent time at in the summer.

Green Lakes is part of the New York State Parks System in Upstate New York. It is an incredibly beautiful park with two very deep lakes formed as plunge pools as melting snow cascaded over the limestone cliffs during the Ice Age some 10,000 to 12,000 years ago. It was here that I learned to swim, to do craft projects, and to box, of all things. Yes, boxing was part of this day camp run by the boxing coach Roy Simmons, Sr. from Syracuse University. I highly doubt that it's a collegiate sport any longer.

Cazenovia Lake, a few miles further south, is where I learned to fish. My parents had a summer camp on the shore of Cazenovia for perhaps two years. We would bring our friends out occasionally for a sleep-over, bonfire, and breakfast in the morning. We weren't there for very long, as I remember, because there wasn't a good area to swim-too many weeds which is still the situation today. They sold that camp for a much better one on Skaneateles Lake in the Finger Lakes Region.

This lake and several others nearby were carved out as the glaciers moved down from Canada. These grooves were filled in by the melting snow to form very deep, very cold lakes running from North to South.

On the property they bought was a small two bedroom cottage which served as base camp for a few years until they had a much larger one built with a large kitchen, dining area, living room, bathroom, and two more bedrooms. We had 150 feet of frontage, clear deep water with no weeds, and acreage behind us to explore and sometimes rent-out to area farmers for hay or alfalfa fields.

It was here at 11 years old that I learned to drive my dad's **International** truck. I had to put a pillow under my butt so that I could see over the steering wheel. We owned the road coming down to camp so basically I wasn't on public property. It was standard shift but that seemed to come naturally to me. By the time I took driver education in high school, I already had been driving for 5 years.

There was plenty to do at camp. We were there for the entire summer. I had a lawn mowing route in town. I'd load the lawnmower on the boat using some planks and unload at the dock in town. I banked over $600.00 for my first summer which I thought was pretty darn good. I learned to water ski and scuba dive using a friend's equipment. We could get down to 40 feet looking for fresh-water mussels. I didn't think the fishing was all that great considering the hours spent and the low return over the many years. My dad still worked in the family business in Syracuse but would leave a list every morning of extra chores that he expected to have done by the time he came home.

After dinner I'd quite often go hunting with my dog, Ginger. Wood chucks were prime meat for that Border collie. There was always swimming, boating, water-skiing, and hiking to keep us occupied. As I became older, I quite often helped the local farmers, the Greenfield brothers, during haying time. Now that was hard work trying to keep your balance on a moving hay wagon while lifting bales of hay up to someone else doing the stacking. This was usually on the hottest and most humid day as well. I learned a lot, most importantly, not to be a farmer when I grew up.

Doctor Widger was the local veterinarian. He not only took care of dogs and cats but he had a daily rural route attending farm animals. My days spent with him meant waking up early at camp, quickly getting a shower and something to eat and then out the door to meet him up at the road. We were usually on the road by 6:30 or 7:00. We'd go from farm to farm taking care of dairy cows, horses, sheep, or whatever animals needed attention. His route for the day was based on calls from farmers received the day before. This is probably my first interest in pursuing a medical career of some sort, but more about that later.

My first real job was working for the lumber yard in town unloading railroad boxcars, painting barns, digging trenches, and whatever else nobody wanted to do. It didn't take long to figure out that I was better suited for a job where I could use my brain rather than my back. Mind you, I'm not putting down manual labor; it just wasn't what I wanted for the rest of my life.

The following summer, in pursuit of medical experience, I got a job as an orderly on floor 2R at St. Joseph's Hospital. I worked there for the next three years when not attending classes in school. I worked pre-op, post-op, emergency room, burn unit, and psychiatric on 3W. I was also, with the help of interns, able to see quite a bit of surgery. They would sneak me in to observe. With a mask on, the surgeon had no idea that I wasn't in med school. It was a very interesting time in my life, one that only a few get to experience. It gave me tremendous compassion for the elderly which would help me later.

A black intern opened my eyes to jazz music—Ahmad Jamal, Dave Brubeck, Thelonius Monk—some of the best. I was to sit about 10 feet from George Shearing while he was playing at the London House in Chicago, years later.

There was one time while working psychiatric that I took five men down to a gym-exercise area to play a game of basketball. We had a good work-out and when I brought them back two hours later, there were city police all over the hospital looking for us. You see, it was a locked ward, and I shouldn't have taken them off the floor. I was new to that area and didn't realize the potential consequences. The hospital staff thought that they had escaped and had taken me hostage. Needless to say the supervisor told me the next day that all five slept like babies that night and they were going to look at exercise as part of the regimen.

Part of the treatment for some patients was electro-shock therapy. The patient was put to sleep with an intravenous drug. Then they were given a muscle relaxant. A gel was swabbed on the legs near the ankles and on the temporal area of the skull. Electrodes were attached to a device which produced an electric current. This would pass through the body to change the brain waves and realign the patient's personality bringing them back to "normal", whatever that is. There wasn't enough current to really harm them but it sure was terrifying to watch. I made darn sure that I acted "normal" for the duration of my life—no zombie existence for me!

We had some great parties out at camp. It was a chance for doctors, nurses, and staff to have some fun for a day. It was a good break from the stress, heartbreak, and death that we experienced every single day.

Politely put, I had to ask a neighbor to return back to his own property one day. He came over to complain that I had invited blacks to my party. I wasn't going to explain the fact that they were doctors and nurses because it wouldn't have mattered to him anyway. It was my house, my party, my friends, my chance to be vocal about his outward prejudice. No explanation was going to be given. I often wondered how he would feel if he had to rely on my friends if a hospital stay was ever necessary.

    I never found out until pre-med at Syracuse University that I had a condition that affects a lot of males, and that's color-blindness. It was during a Saturday morning Anatomy and Physiology lab that I was questioned and tested by a grad student. He was doing a paper on the topic of color-blindness and noticed that my dissection notes were incorrect. He gave me a test and informed me that I had better consider taking something other than medicine. One door closes—another opens! I switched schools and switched my major to Business with a minor in English.

13

CADET LIFE

It's a beautiful sun-shiny day at camp and Dib asks me if I want to go to work with him. We're supposedly on our way to his office but that's not his true intention. Within an hour we're driving through the entrance to the Manlius Military Academy for an admissions test. I'm not asked about this ahead of time, it's something he wants me to do.

I had three wishes in life. One, to have my fingernails pulled out with pliers, two, to walk a mile on hot coals, and three, to go to a military school. I guess only one will come true! In the long run it's probably for the best because I can spend the next five years boarding at a military prep school and be away from my parent's marital problems. They haven't been getting along lately, and I know why. Dib has had a girlfriend for several years and Mom has known about it for some time. Maybe this will be a good break for me from their alternating arguments and silence. Anyway, this will be home for me from 8th grade thru 12th. I have three weeks left of freedom at camp and just a few days to say "goodbye" to my friends.

The first part of September finds me in the lower level of Verbeck Hall on Route 92 in Manlius, NY. This is my barracks where I'll be living until the new barracks is completed across the road, up on the main campus. The first few days will be spent on learning how to polish your brass, "spit-shine" your shoes, and roll your socks in pairs. I don't know why I came so unprepared—I should have known how to do these things at home. Next you have to quickly learn the "chain of command" so you'll know who to salute and who to ignore (that's my version). We proceed to march everywhere and learn that "mess" means food (some days it does). I can't wait until classes start so some sort of normalcy returns.

Classes start a week later and an after school routine of sports is on the agenda. Now we're getting somewhere! This isn't going to be so awful after all! The homesickness has departed and I'm learning what's acceptable and what isn't (this part takes five years). Fall means football and what a team we have! Our junior varsity team plays local high schools and our varsity plays college freshman teams (popular back then, but non-existent now).

The varsity goes undefeated until the last game against Army. The entire school goes to West Point every year for this battle. They take us by a score of 6-0 after a very rough game.

I want you to know that earlier in the season we played Syracuse and beat them! This Syracuse team went on to win the National Championship in 1959, three years later, so you might say that we beat the best! Our team was coached by Tom Cahill and Al (JAB) Vedder. Either could have been head coach, that's how talented they were. Tom went on to coach at Army, and Al coached lacrosse and football at Fayetteville-Manlius H.S. before coaching at Colgate.

The school, I learn, is close to battalion strength, i.e. 4 companies-A, B, C, and H.Q. We have 8 platoons, 32 squads, and over 400+ cadets housed in 3 barracks on 180 acres of property. We all wear the same uniforms, eat the same meals, have the same routine day in-day out—we're all learning how to *kill* others at PMS&T classes—not exactly your normal high school life!

We are inspected every year by the Army to re-evaluate our status. Of all the military academies in the country, we remained #1. This meant that we wore the exact same uniform as the regulars except our insignia was different. From this ranking we could place two cadets in each of the military colleges. More than that number went into other military academies and R.O.T.C. programs in private universities.

Unfortunately, they didn't heed the warnings given about the build-up for Vietnam. A large number of my class did not return, except in body bags. I don't look forward to an upcoming trip to the "Wall" in Washington, D.C. It will be difficult to see names of cadets that I played soccer with, sat next to at meals, or just hung out with in the dayroom watching television. I had my fill of marching after five years so I never signed up for R.O.T.C. at Syracuse.

I still, to this day, have a strong feeling against Jane Fonda, (We're not fond-a Jane), the anti-war rallies and drug use of that period. I know that I would not have liked Woodstock, except for some of the music. Going to see

"Hair" on Broadway in later years, helped me to understand what was going on but it angered me so to see these "hippies" spitting at our troops at the airports as they're returning from Vietnam.

"Jousting With Ignorance Is Like Fighting Windmills"

Michael Suib, a poet and author who drives a cab in Key West, wrote the following which appeared in the *Miami Herald* on Sunday, November 30, 2003:

> "I am en route to the airport with two couples who live somewhere along the New Jersey coast. This day I am driving my van, and the two men occupy the seat directly behind me. The women are in the very rear of the cab placed there by the guys because, as one man so aptly put it, 'I'm too fat to get back there.'
> In our travels, we pass a man wearing faded blue bib overalls who is plodding slowly along on a bicycle, pulling a little cart behind him. He is carrying on an animated conversation with himself and is erratically gesturing to no one in particular with the one free hand he has allowed himself.
> One of the men in my taxi points at him and comments 'Get a look at that Bozo.' The Bozo he is referring to is no such thing, of course. The man is a local, sometimes eccentric, gentleman. He does have his share of problems, and has been known to exhibit some hostility toward the general public. Most of his high jinks though, are fairly benign and primarily verbal. And he is homeless. He has been, he recently told me, for 14 years. He camps in the mangroves around the edges of Key West and is a usual sight pedaling his bicycle along South Roosevelt Blvd. most mornings. The little cart that he tows behind him is stacked snugly with his sleeping gear and other possessions, strapped down and protected from the rain, the sun, and the wind by a tattered tarpaulin.
> For years his only companion was a small dog, a Jack Russell, and the little dog rode happily tucked into the folds of the man's belongings. But ultimately, the little dog, with less tolerance for passersby than his owner, bit a few people and was taken away by the authorities.
> Alone again.
> The handlebars on his bicycle are heavily laden with plastic bags stuffed with clothing and other personal items. His hair, braided in the back, is counter-balanced by a reddish beard that is also braided and festooned with several colorful beads.
> I listen to the rude comment from my passenger and let it pass, excusing it as an isolated instance of stupidity. But when the man persists with another asinine statement about the world being a better place without

'*those people*'—I hate that expression—I come to the homeless man's defense.

'He's a Vietnam vet,' I say quietly.

The men look at me when I make this statement; their eyes glaze over as they turn me out and add me to their list of anonymous people.

Jousting with ignorance can be as frustrating as jousting with windmills, I find. The man on the bicycle has no family and no friends and he seems to like it that way, but of that I am not sure. His only complaint about the world he lost contact with many years ago is that just before the thin glue that held him together gave way, he received a letter from Ed McMahon promising him someone would be knocking on his door soon with a check for a huge sum of money.

He still awaits that day; feeling somehow cheated out of his fortune, and carries that letter, still buried in his personal papers.

There are many such disenfranchised people on the streets of Key West, with no lifeline to family or friends to hang onto or from whom they can seek help: cadres of working people, veterans, mentally and physically disabled, substance abusers, abused women and children. They are all part of our 'One Human Family' who can use a helping hand, and yes, even a handout.

Each year about this time, I am reminded of how lucky I now am, and how fragile that thread of luck is, exactly. Thanksgiving stirs memories for me of sadder times. Holidays away from family and friends, with my only companionship being loneliness and a touch of despair, I remember those occurrences clearly but without nostalgia.

This year, again, we have brigades of young people in harm's way, facing a hostile environment. When they return, they will conceivably be the veterans who will walk our streets 30 years from now and have some clown from New Jersey point a finger at them and comment, 'Hey, get a look at that Bozo.'" (Michael Suib myherald.com)

A replica of the Vietnam Veterans Memorial Wall was on display at the New York State Fairgrounds through this past weekend. Here is a breakdown by age of those killed in combat.

Deaths—total: 58,249   average age: 23.11
Enlisted: 51,651   22.37
Officers: 6,598   28.43

Five men killed in Vietnam were only 16 years old. The oldest killed was 62.

(Source: Combat Area Casualties File, National Archives)

14

MY LIFE FOR THE NEXT FIVE YEARS

A usual day at M.M.A. meant getting up at 6:00, inspection outside at 6:10, and morning mess at 7:00, classes from 9:00 to 12:00. Formation for mess at lunchtime was 12:30 with afternoon classes until 3:00. You either played a sport or reported for physical education from 4:00 until 5:00 (you weren't supposed to carry any extra weight). I was the most physically fit in my life.

Dinner was next, followed by study hall from 7:00 to 9:00. You had free time to call home or hang out in a friend's room or the dayroom until "lights out" at 10:00. That was our day-very structured, *very compliant*.

It certainly was a different world from that of my friends in a normal high school environment. There were no cars allowed, no smoking, no girls on the grounds unless there was a dance, which wasn't often. But, there were no gangs, no "zip" guns, and no tension. It was a good learning environment and I worked hard for good grades, 19th out of a class of 119! We had an incredible faculty. Most were former college professors that wanted to keep teaching, but in a smaller setting. Our classes were limited to 15 to 18 cadets which was ideal for group discussion and one-on-one help.

We had an "unofficial" radio station, *WMAN*, which went on the air at 9:00 almost every night until we felt pressure from the FCC for broadcasting illegally. Our broadcast range was sufficient to reach the local girls in Manlius, Cazenovia, and Fayetteville. This, of course, irritated the hell out of the local guys, "townies", for infringing on their territory.

They retaliated one evening on Halloween by attempting to paint our World War 1 monument, a canon, with some bright orange paint. They were caught and had their clothes removed (everything). They were covered with their own paint, and sent away. I wish I could have heard their explanations when they got home.

Springtime would find them back to test us again. Suburban Park was located across the road from our soccer fields. This was an amusement park that was open in the evening and on weekends. One particular evening we were alerted to the sight of a very large angry group on one of the fields. These were not cadets as we're still in study hall.

Our barracks commander for that particular evening was an ex-Marine whom we called "Iron Balls" because he was the toughest person you'd ever want to meet. "Iron Balls" called over to the other barracks and instructed the other cadets to assemble at our barracks, Farmer Hall, for military tactics instruction "on the double."

The officers split the battalion into three groups. This is all done out of sight of the "townies." Group 1, which I'm in, is called "the bait." Our job is to approach the hostile group but don't engage them. Group 2 and 3 are the older and far bigger cadets who are sent out to surround the "enemy." It works perfectly for within 15 minutes they're outnumbered 6 to 1 with us having a definite advantage. The message was received "loud and clear" that we weren't to be fooled with-*no future problems!*

From the very start of school I could tell that the cadet officers were not well liked by the other cadets. When it came time for OCS (Officer Candidate School) in the summer, I always declined the invitation to attend which annoyed the administration and my dad. The way I looked at it I'd rather have true friends because I was not looking at the military as a long-term option. I guess you could say I was not "gung ho". I had enough rank as a squad leader so that everyone left me alone. The important thing was academics-that's why I was there. It was similar, I suppose, to an Exeter or Andover except they didn't have to march.

I found my niche in sports by playing soccer very well. I was right fullback on defense. Commander Rugh was our coach, my Latin teacher, my advisor, and *my dad away from home*. We would talk by the hour about various situations-one smart man, he was. My mom and my younger sister came to all my games, whether they were home or away, in sunshine or snow, for all 4 years. My dad showed up for one of my games in all those years, but he never missed a football or lacrosse game when my brother was playing. I was glad that at least my brother had support.

I swore that if I ever had children of my own that I would attempt to attend their games, concerts, plays, or recitals. I did, and still do. I even go to high school events that my own children are not participating in. Quite often there are team dinners at the end of the season. Some parents come for the award dinner but don't go to the games. I don't understand their priorities.

15

OUT FOR A STROLL

At the military school we had several clubs that you could join such as Explorers or Hiking. The Explorers was part of Scouts and was entirely medical oriented. On certain Saturdays we joined fellows from other schools to observe surgery at Upstate Medical Center and go to different research facilities in the area. The Hiking Club was geared toward exploration in the Adirondack Mountains. We climbed Mt. Marcy one weekend and the trip was close to a disaster. Our survival training kept us from certain death.

The weather for the weekend was to be bright and clear but cold at night. We brought two vans from school loaded with food and camping gear for a fun-filled time climbing Mt. Marcy and exploring the area. We arrived before noon and set up base camp before heading out. Like I said, it was a beautiful spring day in late May, as I recall, so there wasn't a plan to unpack heavy clothes. We left in shorts, tee shirts, hiking shoes, and lightweight sweatshirts on the Van Hoevenberg Trail to the summit.

The trail looked clear with very little snow all the way to the top. The plan, in case we got separated, was to meet at the summit and wait for remaining members to catch up with the others. We'd spend some time taking pictures and then head back down the same trail to our lean-tos for dinner that night.

Everyone eventually made it to the top but I could tell that some were out of shape and were exhausted already. A short rest should take care of that because it was all down hill from now on. One person of our group convinced others that it would be boring going back the way we came and that we should consider an alternate route for "the fun of it!" He supposedly was very familiar with the area from past hikes years before with a Scout group. It was foolishly decided to follow this new plan.

Down the mountain we went southwest on a new trail that most of us weren't familiar with. The trail markings existed for a while so we knew the general direction in which we were heading. My dead reckoning comes from the observations of the sun and moon. It was turning cloudy and the temperature was dropping rapidly as we're now in the shadow of Skylight Mountain. I'm considering the halt of this plan but others have now moved on too far ahead. Here shortly comes the part where fun turns to panic—snow, and lots of it. It's not out of the sky but already on the ground from the winter storms. It's what is termed "rotten snow." Within a short period of time we are up to our waists in heavy, wet, cold, snow.

We're down in a trough near Lake Tear of the Clouds at what hikers call the Four Corners. I've told you already that we're not prepared for this. At each step we take, we sink in to the point where we're making no progress. Those that were tired before are now really in trouble. Some are starting to give up. My Irish temper comes out to keep them focused on getting the hell out of there.

I'm in shape so maybe if I break trail and lead, it will make it easier on the others. The same guy who suggested this alternate jaunt knows of a ranger cabin in the vicinity where we can stay for the night as it's now pitch black out and you can't see the trees in front of you. We don't have lanterns or flashlights with us. They're back at base camp.

We somehow found the cabin, broke in and started a fire to warm up. There are a few dry pairs of socks for those who are already experiencing frostbite. Snow is gathered to make tea as we found tea bags, but no food. The night is spent with different feet under my armpits to keep their circulation going. My thanks go out to the interns that I learned from during those summers at the hospital. Shoes and clothing are placed in front of the fire to hopefully dry before the morning.

There is no way to communicate our peril to the outside world as there's no phone in the cabin. We're just going to tough it through before conditions get worse—and they do! We pass Gray Peak and Lake Tear of the Clouds in the morning on our way to Opalescent River where we turn and head north back to Marcy Dam. All along these water ways I remove my shoes, tie the laces together, and hang them around my neck—I'll need them later and I want them dry. It's a long way out and there are times I have to carry one of the cadets on my back because he is having a hard time walking because of frostbite. We're now walking on a trail that is totally under water from the spring thaw. It's ice cold but I know we have to keep moving.

We finally arrived later at base camp only to find that we still had no food. Apparently while we were gone overnight, a bear or raccoon found our food supply and tore it all apart. Several are in need of medical attention and we're all starving so we head off to find the hospital and a restaurant. Those in the worst condition are left behind in Saranac and the balance of us return to school.

As we pull up the main driveway from our excursion to the High Peaks, everyone is forming up for our Sunday drill on the parade grounds. They're all lined up in dress blues with an elegant crowd watching as we pile out looking like "death warmed over." I need a shower badly and then a check-up at the school infirmary. Dinner that night of mediocre food actually tasted pretty good. Surprising how an event like that can change your attitude.

I had been up in the Adirondacks many times before, mostly at the Lake Placid Club. My parents were members and we'd try to go on vacation there every other year. My younger sister, brother, and I were all speed-skaters and the LPC had a great outdoor rink. It was built as a training center for the 1932 Olympics.

Jacque Susann, who it's reported is the father of the well-known author, Jacqueline Susann, brought his dogsled team to the LPC to give rides around the property to the members. He's an interesting character who lives on a farm outside of town near North Elbe. This is where John Brown of Civil War fame is buried.

Mount Van Hoevenberg is another venue close by. That's where they have the bobsled run which I'm lucky enough to have ridden on several years later with the world-famous driver from Italy, Eugenio Monte. He was making practice runs and I was fortunate to be in the #3 spot just in front of the brakeman. It took quite awhile to get to the top by truck, but literally seconds to arrive at the finish line as we were barreling at more than 90 mph.

Just a few years later the Kennedy family was to spend some time at the LPC but it was rumored that the club was anti-Semitic in their club membership. The Kennedy family changed their arrangements and stayed across the lake, in the village. When my parents read the article about this in the paper, they dropped their membership at LPC.

16

EUROPE

In the summer of 1958, my family took off in different directions—not planned that way but just how it happened. My brother, Bill, was on a cross-country trip to California with a Manlius Military school group chaperoned by two teachers.

Joan, Linda, Mom, and Dib are off on a trip to the Maritime Provinces—Nova Scotia, Newfoundland, New Brunswick, and Prince Edward Island. I'm off to Montreal to board the *QSS Arcadia* crossing the North Atlantic to Southampton, England.

We embarked on the morning of June 27th down the St. Lawrence River to the ocean. As I recall, the crossing over took six days and the return trip was seven. On five of the six days we experienced 35 to 40 foot swells. Needless to say, it doesn't take long for seasickness to take over. My comfort zone was up-top where there's plenty of cold, fresh air to breathe. I'm not going to describe the conditions down below—it's up to your imagination! Being "topside," as they say, I saw flying fish, whales, sharks, and icebergs. I prayed that they had plenty of early-warning devices on board, better than what the *Titanic* carried.

The crossing was well worth it though, when we finally arrived at Ireland. A small ferry from Cork, came out to pick up a few passengers as the harbor is small and too shallow for our draft. I find it hard to describe the beauty of this island after seeing nothing but water for the better part of a week.

Departing Ireland, we headed for the port of Southampton, England. We won't see this ship again for several weeks. We're quickly off to tour museums, churches, Bath, Stratford-on-Avon, London, Sherwood Forest, Stonehenge and all the other places that tourists should see. Then we're on our way to the major cities of Scotland for four days of solid rain!

From there we cross by boat to Norway. This is an absolutely gorgeous country that you have to see for yourself. All of Scandinavia is beautiful, for that matter. A three day hike in the mountains is planned from Finse to Aurland.

The plan is to stay at youth hostels along the way. There is a quick map meeting in the morning indicating the hike for day #1—I hope this is better than the Marcy trip. Here's the part my buddies back home don't believe. Starting out on the trek there are three girls who want to join our group so they're not going it alone. As it turns out they are chorus girls from Bergen, and I don't mean singers!

The first section of the hike is a long one but I'm in shape, so it's not that bad. At the hostel everything is ready for us—a warm bed, a hearty meal, and great comradeship with students and travelers from other countries. Later that evening, while the night owls are still sitting around the fire, these three gals suggest a swim in the lake. It's the time of year there when it's daylight nearly all the time but extremely cold at night, so I decline in favor of the fire. What a mistake! Six other young people join them out front whereupon all three girls take off all their clothes and jump in followed by the others. This is my very first experience seeing a girl naked and there's still two more days left of the hike. My second time is coming up in Paris.

We are traveling to Oslo next and then on to Copenhagen, Denmark. We rented scooters and had a great time exploring the sandwich and pastry shops during the day and going to the Tivoli Park at night. Then we enter Germany but that will be covered in the third part of this book.

Next we go to the small country of Luxembourg and then to the World's Fair in Brussels, Belgium. It has been 46 years since this trip so you'll have to bear with me about the details of this travelogue. France is the last country that we tour. Versailles, Norte Dame, Louvre, Arch de Triumphe, and the Seine are as beautiful as everyone says but the people are the rudest I've ever met. You would think that all we've done for the French in two world wars and considering the millions of dollars they still owe our country, that their attitude would be better.

Our headquarter hotel is in the Latin Quarter. One night we go to the Lido, the other to the Follies! Colonel Chase and his wife, Judith, tell us that it's all a part of our education. From my studies, the girls in France look just like those I saw in Norway only with more makeup on, nothing else!

The last leg of our journey is a train ride through the Normandy countryside to the port of Cherbourg where we catch the *Arcadia* back to Montreal. This part of France is very interesting as I can visualize our troops liberating this area during the end of the war. Parts of the villages have yet to be repaired from the fighting that took place here. Now that I like history, I'd like to return again.

17

DOWN SOUTH

The CQ (charge of quarters) in the barracks came upstairs to tell me that I have a phone call. This is a puzzle because I never get calls during the week. Mom is on the phone and wants to know how quickly I can pack some clothes. I explain to her that I just can't leave when I want to. We get two 6 hour passes per month but they can only be used on weekends. She tells me that she has already cleared it with the headmaster because we are to be gone for two weeks or so and she'll explain later, as if I don't already know.

She has booked the two of us on a trip into the Deep South. We are going by bus; she needs me to come along as a learning experience and to be her security as she won't travel alone. Mom tries to explain that things aren't going so well at home and she needs to "get away." She feels that my grades are good and that it shouldn't be a problem catching up when we get back. I give her confidence that I'm there for her, but I don't let on that I already know the circumstances, all too well.

This is the pre-Civil Rights era before all hell breaks loose. The bus stops have "white only" bathrooms, "white only" drinking fountains, "white only" counters. When blacks are traveling down there, where do they eat, get a glass of water, or use restroom facilities? They're obviously treated as sub-humans. It doesn't make life easier that the locals notice license plates on the bus are from New York. You can feel the hatred through your skin. Now I know what those three "freedom riders" must have felt just a few years later. Mom taught me to try to be accepting of all people no matter their race or religion. I hope now that feelings have changed for the better. If attitudes haven't changed, we're no further ahead.

The trip takes us through Pennsylvania, West Virginia, Virginia, North and South Carolina, Georgia, and Florida on the way down. We also visit D.C. and Delaware on the return trip.

I'm the youngest on board and I have nothing in common with the senior citizens. Mom is the second youngest! The rural South is very poor and appears to me to be quite backward at times. The cities process the products grown nearby i.e. tobacco, corn, sweet potatoes, cotton, and sugar cane. I've been to Florida before but rapidly by train or plane. So, you see, she has accomplished two things at the same time—a break for her and new experiences for me.

Hopefully, she was in a far better frame of mind when we returned.

18
1961

I would be remiss if I didn't mention our "still" that we set up in "the cave" which was under the railroad tracks behind the school. We had cooked our own mash and had "borrowed" Doc Williams copper tubing from his chemistry lab for the coils. We must have done it properly for none of us got sick or went blind! Chemistry classes weren't a total waste, I guess. It shows what you can accomplish when you have a little extra time on your hands. I always remind my own children that if they do even half of what I got involved in, they'll turn out okay.

My mom always wished they had Velcro back then. When you get "busted" for doing something contrary to the rules, you would usually loose a stripe as a demotion and have to march "extra duty". So my mom would remove them only to sew them back on again later. She could have affixed **Velcro** to the stripes had it been available back then.

My brother ended up as Battalion Commander two years later and I was very proud of him. Even though he had more rank, I always tell him that I had more fun. Quite possibly, that's how I got some attention from my dad.

The rest of military school went by uneventfully and graduation came in June of 1961. One of my roommates was from Caracas, Venezuela—I never saw him again. My other roommate never overcame his feelings of depression which later, I learned, lead to his suicide—I never saw him again either. Many more died overseas in Nam, approximately 11% of our classmates, but there are still no plans for a memorial. Class reunions never amounted to much. I sense that they're just looking for alumnae money. Anti-war feelings in the country led to the demise of military schools. If I remember correctly, ours closed in 1970.

I live less than a mile from the campus and have offered several times to conduct tours but it always falls on deaf ears. I feel that I have something to contribute to their memory, but it seems that nobody gives a shit. Pay attention to the next parade you watch—hardly anyone claps for Vietnam vets, I do! Life moves on—just another chapter.

I'd like to share an article with you about a cadet I briefly knew about at the Manlius Military Academy. The source follows the article:

"I would like to address my remarks to the younger journalists, those who will soon be leaving school. You will be the ones who will bear the responsibility of this profession for years to come.

I would like to touch on some of the broader aspects of our profession namely, what you can expect when you leave school to become an editor or reporter.

Several years ago the Army football coach devised a new offense where one end stayed at an extreme side of the field and sometimes didn't even come to the huddle between plays. Sports writers dubbed him 'the lonesome end.' He was part of the team but remote from it. He was part of the action but divorced from it.

The lonesome end was Cadet Bill Carpenter. He played his position perfectly and followed through in real life because he was decorated with the nation's second highest award for bravery. In Vietnam as a captain, he called down fire on his own position when it looked as though it would be overrun by the Vietcong.

The image of the lonesome end in football was criticized particularly in the middle of the week when the sports writers don't have anything else to write about. But Carpenter didn't worry about his image at West Point or in Vietnam…"

Wes Gallagher, General Manager of the Associated Press 3/2/00
The Nieman Foundation for Journalism at Harvard University
(www.nieman.harvard.edu/reports/99-4)

Bill Carpenter was a cadet at the Manlius Military Academy before attending West Point.

19

COLLEGE LIFE

I was accepted at Syracuse University among other schools but I had been away from home for the past five years and I thought that was enough. Commander Rugh, my advisor, wanted me to go to Hunter College in New York City. I should have listened to him because Syracuse was not a good fit for me and the marital issues at home were far worse than before. I spent a great deal of time at the library so I wouldn't have to listen to their arguments. Class sizes were large and very impersonal. There was no exchange with professors and I had a feeling that I really didn't belong.

I experienced what I call, "reverse discrimination" in my freshman year. I was dating a Jewish girl. Her name was Alice and she was in my pre-med classes. When Parents Weekend was near I asked her to go to dinner with my family. She said that she had other plans and might just go home for the weekend. As it turned out, she and her family and a Jewish guy from our class ended up at the same restaurant that evening. She was mortified when we walked in, but I introduced her to my parents anyway. The following Monday after classes she stopped me outside to try and explain what happened. It seems that her parents would not have understood that she was dating someone outside of the faith. It was okay for me to have a Jewish room mate at military school, but not to date a Jewish girl, I guess. We remained just friends after that and went our separate ways.

One of my daughters married a Jewish fellow, and a son married a Jewish girl so it appears as though some things have changed for the better. The world is changing; we shouldn't let race, creed, or color be a reason to walk away from a relationship.

One class, not selected by me, was a conversational French class and I never had taken French in my life. This teacher was pre-occupied with flirting with the girls in the class rather than conjugating verbs. He probably was old enough to be their father. I reminded him at the end of the semester that, "18 will get you 20." He got the message, I hope.

They had your money and you were on your own—welcome to the real world! It was partly my own fault for not doing well there because I couldn't handle all of this new-found freedom after five years of a very regimented (no pun intended) life. I left after seven months and had to bring some incompletes with me which I finished later in night school.

Onondaga Community College opened up the following year and that is where I transferred. It is basically the same style that I was used to—small classes with lots of individual attention but still in a college environment. I met my first wife there as well as some really great teachers.

"Mrs. Sawyer, this book is partially dedicated to you. In creative writing class, you told me that one day I would write something of value and here I am, thanks to your critique. I hope that you're pleased."

You'd think my dad would be proud of two semesters on the dean's list and two on honors, but not one word—I stopped trying to please him. I don't think he even came to my graduation—his loss! It was a challenge handling married life, college, and a job at the same time, but lots of people do it.

One afternoon as I'm getting ready to pull into the school parking lot there are two girls crossing the street listening to a transistor radio. They are apparently on the same frequency that I am on. Both let out a scream and start crying as I also hear that John F. Kennedy, our President, has been killed. Classes are called off for the rest of the week and our lives are changed, forever. It's a very turbulent time with assassinations of Malcolm X, Martin Luther King, and Robert Kennedy to follow.

20

JOE BURNS' LEGACY

"Dear Natalie, Jasmin, Laurin, Sarah, and Sabrina,

Enclosed is a cut-glass dish that I would like to give you to put on your dresser to hold special items or possibly jewelry when you get older. Please save this letter because I have a story to tell you and I want to write it now while it is fresh in my memory. You know how older people tend to forget details.

A very long time ago some of your relatives came to this country from Ireland. They were the O'Byrne family from County Mayo in the south-western part of the country. They left the harbor port of Cork on a steamer going to New York City. There was a potato famine and everybody was starving. They had just enough money to pay for their tickets to the United States. New York was supposed to be the city of opportunity and they heard that the streets were paved in gold.

When they arrived over here after many days on the ocean, they found that conditions were not that much better than what they had left in Ireland except that here they could work in menial jobs and buy some food. There was prejudice against the Irish and they found it necessary to change the family name to Burns which would partially hide their ancestry.

To feel more comfortable in New York, different people had a tendency to group together because of common foods, language, culture, etc. The Burns family moved into an Irish neighborhood called

Hell's Kitchen. There were also Italian families living there on the lower west side. This set up a lot of friction for both groups.

Mr. Burns decided that this was not where he wanted his family to live. He eventually moved everybody to a farm just outside of Honesdale, Pa. This is where my grand-father, Joseph Edward Burns, became an apprentice in one of the many cut-glass factories. There were 13 factories in operation at that time all in one city. It was the cut-glass capital of the United States.

Joe Burns learned quickly how to cut Brilliant patterns. He eventually became partners with a man named Hoare and they set-up business in the Elmira-Corning area of New York State. Besides cutting glass, Joe Burns represented the Norton Company which made the grind stones used to cut the glass. He traveled all over the states and eventually settled in Canastota, NY with his wife and his daughter, Bobette, who was my mom. So at this part of the story we have covered three generations already.

In Canastota, he was asked to teach employees of the Ideal Glass Co. how to cut different patterns that he learned over the years. The one that he was best known for was the *'Diamond Poinsettia,'* which is the one on the dish that I am giving to you. He moved his business to Syracuse when the Ideal Co. closed due to financial problems. He continued on his own until May of 1919 when he switched over to making serrated-edged knives.

So, there is a brief family history on the Burns side of the Edgerton family. The dish is not only sentimental, but it has value also. Please pass it on some day. Thank you.

Love,

Grandpa

This was written recently to my grand-daughters when I gave each of them a cut-glass dish made by their great-grandfather, Joe Burns. He moved his business to Water Street in the city. We were advised a few years ago that we are one of twelve companies that were originally located on the Erie Canal to be still in business today. I've been a third generation manager-owner for the past 43 years.

At one time we manufactured some products and purchased others for resale. For the past 30 years, our concentration has been on importing kitchen knives, barbeque sets, and kitchen gadgets from Japan, Taiwan, China, Thailand, and most currently, Brazil.

The original business operation was situated downtown and later moved further out to the 1200 block of Water St. as they needed more room for production.

I remember going down to the factory on Saturday mornings with my dad to reload the furnace with coal for the weekend. Bill and I each had our own small shovel to help him. The floors were dirt and the machines were driven by wide belts which were attached to an overhead steel shaft that ran the entire length of the building. There were drying bins of sawdust which were usually inhabited by mice that came in to get warm and raise their little ones. The shipping room was in the front, near the street, where trucks would pick up shipments going all over the country. The serration wheels were in the back where the grinders were busy all day turning out thousands of dozens of stock. These workers were on piece-rate so they had to work fast; the others were on an hourly rate.

The patents had expired in 1936 so we no longer had protection and we now had to compete with all the other knife manufacturers. With costs escalating, we took the unpopular route of the time and started importing. This was anti-union but I felt that if the union shops we were buying from couldn't stay competitive we had our own survival on the line. This turned out to be our salvation as the merchandise coming in from the Orient was every bit as good and much less expensive. Over there, a production week is 54 hours which is 6 days, 9 hours per day! There are very few unions except in larger cities. There is loyalty—both ways.

We could have items made exclusively for us. A product line of maybe 30 items developed into a 24 page catalog in full color with a distribution of 20,000 catalogs per year to our wholesale distributors. It was positive growth from the original 8,500 customers. We needed to move again for growth reasons and neighborhood issues.

21

CONFRONTATIONS

He was born on January 15, 1929 in Atlanta. I met him in Chicago at the Palmer House Hotel on August 26, 1966, and on April 5, 1968 he was assassinated in Memphis. His name was Martin Luther King, Jr. and I met him on the 6th floor in the hotel while attending a trade show. He was there for what, I later learned, was a secret meeting with Mayor Daley. As fate would have it, I was the only one waiting at the freight elevator to go downstairs to get some lunch. The other elevators were packed and I figured that few people knew about this one. He was counting on this also.

He came up with what appeared to be several bodyguards. He was smiling and very cordial to me when he came off the elevator. I think he felt I was part of the mayor's staff until we got talking and I explained why I was there. He explained in short terms that he was trying to get rid of slum conditions in Chicago and that nobody needed to know that he was there.

Within two or three minutes, the elevator doors opened again and this encounter was anything but cordial. The Mayor was a very gruff and brusque individual who seemed to want to be anyplace other than this meeting. His bodyguards were confrontational and left me feeling uneasy.

I didn't realize what an impact this Dr. King would have on people, no matter the color of their skin. His death in 1968 set off firestorms and rioting in Washington, D.C. which quickly spread to 129 other cities, Syracuse being one of them. We were quickly involved in violent rioting, and fires were consuming entire city blocks. The fires and looting were one block from our building and the firemen and policemen were exhausted from working around the clock. When the trucks were going down the street, blacks were throwing rocks and bricks at them, so police escorts were ordered. Plywood was bolted on to the trucks to act as shields.

What was really strange was that they were torching their own homes as well as local businesses. This was sheer stupidity! Where would they live and shop in the coming months?

Water Street became a staging area for the police and fire department. Volunteers were coming in to help spell the regulars. We were providing coffee and snacks to those out front.

A police sergeant asked me if I was a hunter and I thought this was an odd question until I understood his meaning. He explained that they were short of personnel and they were "unofficially" asking local property owners to assist in the protection of their own buildings.

My dad said he'd watch the building during the day if I'd take the night shift. We sent the factory workers home for their own protection, so the building was essentially vacant. I couldn't leave my dad alone so I returned with a revolver and a shotgun that I used for hunting deer. I thank the good Lord that I didn't have to use them.

The front of the building was all windows so the rioters could easily see me in a chair perched on top of a desk. They could also see that I meant business if they threatened us or our building. They would walk by at night and laugh at me or taunt me. Buckshot was loaded first followed by deer slugs in a 6 shot Remington 12 gauge. If that wasn't effective, my Ruger .357 magnum was boss.

Martin Luther King was interested in ending segregation in a non-violent way. The riots and property destruction set his cause back many years. This was not the way he would have wanted to be remembered. According to filed police reports, the arrested were drunken, black males. He would have been very sad to learn this. I've recently read that another in attendance, at that famous meeting in Chicago, was Rev. Jesse Jackson, a rising member of Dr. King's SCLC staff. (soulofamerica.com)

It wasn't long before the area went "down hill" rapidly. One day, Chris, my youngest son, and I had spent the better part of the day squirrel hunting out in the country and I happened to notice that he needed new boots for the winter. I suggested we stop at the Army-Navy Store on the way home and look for new ones. This store is less than two blocks from our building.

On the way out of the store my son noticed a fight down the street. I at first thought that it was just a couple arguing, but on second look I noticed that a black male was trying to steal a white girl's purse. He was pulling on the strap and slapping her in the face trying to get the purse away. At this point we're already in my truck driving over to help her. I yelled at the guy to leave her alone. So he starts swearing at me and walks over to my truck while he's pulling out a spring-activated knife with threatening gestures. Within seconds, he's nose-to-nose with my revolver and I'm sure at this point, he needs a change of underwear.

He dropped the knife and took off running toward the University section with us in hot pursuit. My son is on the phone with 911 asking for police assistance. I'm keeping track of this guy who is trying hard to evade us as I'm calling out street names to the police dispatcher. We can hear the sirens and we're told they'll take over as they have spotted him running between two apartment houses.

As if this wasn't enough, I'm called out of my office one day by our shipping clerk to go in the warehouse, quickly. I can hear an argument and I find two black males in the rear of the building confronting my female workers. When I asked them what they wanted, they told me they were looking for work. I informed them that if they wanted an application they had to go back out the way they came in and go around to the office. They said they were going to "look around" to see if this was a good place to work.

What they were looking for were purses they could steal. Out of sight was an employee who was unwrapping knives for serration. She grabbed the biggest knife she could find and came running at them. These two guys must have been sprinters on their high school track team for they showed us how fast they could run—away!

With more than half the area burned to the ground along with the crap that was happening around us, we decided to sell to the Federal Government for an urban renewal project, whatever that meant. They paid us off, we moved out of the city and off the tax rolls, the building was leveled, and nothing was "renewed".

The area was never developed and that was 34 years ago. It doesn't make any sense to me to drive through this once viable, commercial neighborhood and see vacant lots with weeds growing where buildings once stood. Businesses, like ours, moved to safer "parks" outside the city. The burned-out stores never rebuilt. If you're not wanted, why stay?

The city is dying and the politicians can't figure out what to do! I don't have the answers but unless it's addressed quickly we're in for major problems down the road. There's far too much polarization—whites live in suburbia and have good schools. Most blacks live in the city and some turn to drug sales to get by. Gang wars are prevalent, fathers of black children aren't home to establish positive role models, teenage pregnancy is rampant, drop-out rates are high, and the crime scene is no longer confined to the downtown. The city now has the County Sheriff's Department and the NYS Police assisting on patrols as they can't seem to handle it by themselves. Welfare is a way of life—the more children, the more money. Education is paramount if anything is to be accomplished.

Here are the most current figures of income in relation to levels of education according to the U.S. Census Bureau:
No diploma—$18,734
High School diploma—$27,915
Bachelor's degree—$51,206
Advanced degree—$74,706
But some, I'm sure would scoff at these figures in comparison to what they're bringing in from illicit drug sales.

In our local paper, *The Post Standard*, dated 3/10/05, there is an Associated Press article titled, "More Black Men Die Early...." In the article by David R. Williams of the University of Michigan and Pamela Braboy Jackson of Indiana University, "One reason for the differences is that gains in health care access generally have not included black men unless they were older or disabled, when Medicare became law, the average black man did not live long enough to become eligible. Other factors include the relatively low incomes of black men compared with whites, a rise in gun-related deaths among blacks, blacks' disproportionately high death rate from AIDS, and higher rates of heart disease and diabetes."

I lived in the city for 19 years but I'd never go back. My old neighborhood that I spoke about is rapidly becoming a war zone. One former neighbor was shot in the head and killed because some "coke-head" thought he had some money—some is right-$40.00. He was taken into the basement of his own home and shot in the head, execution style.

Houses and cars are burglarized on a daily basis. Drive-by shootings are in the paper constantly. In the local paper just the other day, I noticed 43 indictments handed up by the Grand Jury. Of the 43, 8 were for men with a residence within ½ mile of my old house on Ridgeway!

The malls of today are the "downtown" of yesterday. I like to just sit and "people watch" while my wife spends her money. The kids move around like zombies with no particular agenda. In talking with security guards, I get the impression, based on their experience, that the malls are just areas where kids can get into trouble with fights, shop-lifting, and gang activity. One mall has a zero tolerance for kids under 18 after 5:00 pm. which just prompts them to go to another.

I prevented a purse-snatching two years ago. As this guy was reaching for my wife's purse, I quickly let him know that the police would have to pick him up off the floor and put him in a basket. His friend wisely suggested a quick departure.

Just this past summer when my wife was at an evening business meeting, I decided to go to an outdoor concert at one of the city parks. I drove in from the suburbs and took a route in the city that I've been on hundreds of times. Not thinking, I drove down a territorial road on the turf between three gangs, Boot Camp, 110, and Elk Block as they call themselves.

Midland Avenue, which is home to these different drug gangs, is intersected by Colvin Street. With my luck, I'm at this intersection when the light turned red and I'm stuck there when a gun battle broke out. The car in front of me won't move so I put the "pedal to the metal", as the expression goes, and I passed around it.

When I got to the park where the concert would be held, there were two police officers on duty by their patrol car. I explained what had just happened but they don't seem too interested. They know where I've been and that this type of occurrence happens almost daily. I'm told there's no use calling it in because the gangs will immediately scatter and will be long gone by the time any law enforcement arrive. One says, "Let them shoot each other, what do we care?" With that statement, therein lies part of the problem. Needless to say, I took an alternate route home.

As if you haven't read enough already, two more confrontations involve white people, one a neighbor, the other, a janitor at our building.

About 8:00 p.m. on a summer evening there's loud pounding on the front door. Pulling away from the television, there's a young girl from across the street crying and screaming hysterically on our porch. All I have to hear is the word "knife" and I brought her inside. I yelled to my family to get upstairs, lock the door and not to come down for anything. When I got across the street I saw the father chasing his son around the car in a drunken rage with a large knife in his hand. The son was in sports in school so I wasn't immediately concerned about the dad catching him considering the condition the dad was in. I told the boy to keep his distance and that I would go and get the police. He told me to hurry because the father expressed a desire to kill the whole family. Now my thoughts go to the mom who, I assume, is inside the house. I don't dare go in there or I could be trapped.

When I got back to my house I called the operator and said that I needed an open line to any police agency available as I had an immediate need, to avoid a possible stabbing. Now the dad is at our house pounding on the door telling me to send his daughter out or I'll be "sorry." That isn't going to happen! At this point I can hear sirens and so does he, as he bolts across the street. Down the street comes the chief of police in an unmarked car. His response was almost instantaneous because he was close by.

He drove his car on the neighbor's lawn and chased him into the house. I couldn't see what was happening but more police from different agencies were quickly arriving. It took six big men to subdue this guy and get handcuffs on him. They took him to jail and an ambulance took the police chief, who was first on the scene, to the hospital. In the house there had been a struggle and both of his hands were cut open as a result of trying to get the knife away.

A few years later I was doing the inventory count at work; the figures didn't gel with what came in the door vs. what has been sold and shipped. We were short! Herb, one of our key employees, told me that I might want to check out a local flea market.

His wife had seen, what appeared to be our merchandise, for sale at a booth there. The following weekend I went to check it out and, sure enough, she was right! I didn't want to arouse suspicion but when I asked the man about the merchandise, he wasn't cooperative. He was though in a few minutes, when the police arrived.

He was arrested and put in the police car for a ride to the station for booking. I was asked to sit in the front seat and the arrested man was in the back. During the conversation in the car, a name came up that was familiar to me. He went on to say that he bought the items from this individual at a very low price. The "seller" turns out to be our janitor who recently switched, at his request, to cleaning our offices on weekends rather than during our office hours—how convenient for him! The arrested man is released pending a later hearing and an arrest warrant is issued for the janitor. Here's where the story gets interesting.

It seems that the janitor and his wife are not getting along and in a phone call to me a few days later she tells me that she has moved out to live with her sister. The wife has a restraining order warrant issued against him about the same time my warrant comes out. I'm told that I should be careful as he's prone to be violent towards her and she wants to warn me about him. He apparently has a flip side to his" born-again" Christianity. He would tell me over the past few months how religious he was and that he loved his fellow man. He apparently just didn't love his wife.

At 3:00 a.m. the following morning the phone rings at home and I'm awakened by a female voice asking me some odd questions—who is at home, do I know so-and-so, are the doors locked?, etc. The New York State Police are trying to quickly determine our safety. The janitor, during the night, found out where his wife was staying, shot and killed her then told relatives that I was next.

The State Police were quickly moving us to a safe house that night. An unmarked car was on the way. I was told to make sure that all ground floor doors and windows were closed and locked. She asked if I had a weapon and if so to locate it but keep clear of windows. Some of us were at home; some were at our summer house on the St. Lawrence River. They had two places to watch. We were moved to a friend's house in a different neighborhood for the night. The guy was captured in the morning and is serving a sentence in prison.

These have been exciting parts of my life but now I'll settle for the dull.

An old Crow Indian saying is, "One has to face fear or forever run from it." I personally have never started a fight—but I've finished some!

I've been fortunate enough to have served on jury duty four times—two criminal cases and two civil cases. Should you ever get a chance to serve, don't pass it up unless it's a celebrity trial in California. The defense attorneys for O.J. Simpson, Michael Jackson and Robert Blake can be happy, however, that I wasn't on those juries.

I have also spent the better part of a day touring Auburn Prison. These two experiences in conjunction with a ten week civilian police academy have reinforced my opinion that the law does work (sometimes) and is still worthwhile. I now have a reinforced respect for law enforcement and the role they play in protecting us.

22

BEING A DAD

The Lord has blessed me with 8 (no typo) wonderful children in my life. As of this writing I'm also a proud grandpa of five granddaughters and one grandson. The kids are spread out now from New Fairfield, Connecticut to Brea, California and down to Leesburg, Virginia. Six are out of college, one is at Marist in Poughkeepsie, and the caboose is a junior in high school. I wish that they all lived closer but that's what happens as they marry and move away to job opportunities.

I really don't know where the time has gone—the oldest is 42, the youngest 16. Random thoughts keep coming back of Cub Scouts, dance recitals, volleyball games, Blue Birds, outdoor track meets, Webelos, school plays, First Communions, Little League, school concerts, lacrosse games, Confirmations, soccer games, Girl Scouts, PTA meetings, graduations, wrestling matches, Brownies, marching band, National Honor Society, college applications and visits, proms, engagements, weddings, and birth announcements.

I had to catch an earlier flight out of Chicago one time to catch my daughter's soccer game. It seems the team figured out that during the regular season if I was there—they won, if I couldn't make it to the game—they lost! They were in a sectional game for the championship and were excited when I finally showed up—they won!

Having a family business was beneficial for all of us. The children could work in the warehouse while on vacation to earn some extra money while at the same time I was teaching them to have a good work ethic and to become achievers. Who knows, someday one of them might be a 4th generation entrepreneur.

Being a dad brings a lot of responsibility with the territory. You have to provide not only for their basic needs of food, clothing, shelter, religious education, and schooling, but lots of understanding and love. Along with this, they have the right to respect and happiness in their lives.

I'm doing the best I can—there are no classes on being a good parent. I've probably made many mistakes along the way. I know that I have large erasers on my pencils and I've put my foot in my mouth so many times that I'm now wearing mint-flavored shoes.

"Before I got married, I had 8 theories about bringing up children. Now I have 8 children and no theories." (Lord Rochester)

During Christmas break of 1982, I had enough of what was supposed to be, "matrimonial bliss." The toughest decision in my entire life, after 20 years of marriage, was how to tell my children that in the morning I would be leaving the house and would not be returning to ever live there again. My first wife and I were "untying the knot" and we were seeking attorneys to work out a legal separation "agreement," if that's what you can call it. My word for it would be signing a "truce" stipulating financial agreements and child care arrangements.

Divorce proceedings would come rapidly thereafter—joint custody of the minors and visitation rights agreed upon. I moved out to find an apartment that I could afford and my oldest son joined me two days later to live with me. Needless to say, it was a big adjustment for everyone. I offered counseling to all the kids but none took me up on it. I guess they all dealt with it in their own way.

Our lives were torn apart and for some it would take years to be able to move on, some still haven't. Some are still angry. I wanted somehow to tell them that I was divorcing their mother—not them! Being apart, I could only provide quality time not quantity time. Christmas was not the same to me for many years to come.

We had separated for a brief period ten years earlier but the same issues kept coming back—nothing changed.

You live the life you're given. You can't look back and beat yourself up over decisions made at the time. I thought it through and hoped that what I was doing was best in the long run. I still today don't regret it.

"Yesterday is history, today is reality, tomorrow is up to the Lord." (Jack Edgerton 2005)

I'm learning to adapt to life's changes. The older children, by the previous marriage, are closer in age. Perhaps I wasn't so patient back then with so many young ones to attend to at the same time. It was hard running two businesses simultaneously then coming home to switch hats to that of a husband-caretaker and father. It took several years to clear military organization and discipline out of my head. Tempers at times ran short. For that, I'm sorry. It's a balancing act that eventually wears on you unless you have a strong resolve and dedication to accomplish the work, while still motivating your children and trying to lead them in the right direction.

You can only lead them so far—they'll make plenty of wrong decisions, as we all do. Sometimes you learn by failure. Hopefully, they see that your values were acceptable so they'll make sound decisions on their own. You can "mother" but you shouldn't "smother" and try not to be a helicopter parent—always "hovering around."

There comes that time in their life, like a young bird, that they have to try their wings. You know from experience that they'll either hit the ground, or soar to new heights. Even the mother bird can't do it for them. Either I was a good dad or not-so-good, all I could do was try. They always say, "the older the child, the bigger the problem." When they have children of their own, it's pay-back time.

> As a young girl, Mackenzie wrote:
> I am one of eight
> Being the seventh is sometimes great.
> My dad has been through a whole lot
> Raising that many—he knows what to do
> and what not.
> My mom, however, had only my little sister and I
> There is still so much she knows and I don't know why.
> Sit us around a table together
> The stories go on, they last forever.
> Many I hear, I have heard once before

Intended to teach me something
What else are big brothers and sisters for?

Chelsea writes:
Mom and Dad—
Thanks! That word pretty much sums up everything you've ever done for me. From helping me grow up to respecting my needs and wants, you've always been there. At times, I know I tend not to show my appreciation for everything, but it's always there, even if I don't know it yet. Now with Kenzie going to college, you're my only inspiration and will be the main people I look up to. So thank you for that.

To all my friends, you've been the cool parents that let me do what I want without harsh restrictions. You're the second parents to all of them and I thank you for that also. You're also the loving parents who have made me who I am today. Thanks—such a simple word yet it means so much.

All my love—Chelsea

A note from Chris on Father's Day:
The ten things Dads want most in life, and # 1 on the list—Less SHIT from their kids!

It is very rewarding to know that they've all had an excellent education and good health. They've married loving and caring spouses and have homes of their own. What more could you ask for? Hodding Carter wrote, "There are only two lasting bequests we can hope to give our children. One of these is roots; the other, wings."

Barbara Streisand sings on the tape, *Higher Ground*, that "there are reasons for the path we take, there are no mistakes, just lessons to be learned."

23

BUSINESS BENEFITS

Syracuse, New York to Narita, Japan is about a 15 hour flight depending on what airline route you take. My business was such that I needed to travel there every other year on buying trips. Japan produced kitchen knives; Bangkok, Thailand was my source for teak items; Hong Kong and Taiwan were known for giftware.

The trips would be of a 3 to 3 ½ week duration and always with a stop-over in Hawaii for a few days of rest on the return trip home.

I had four incredibly loyal, honest, and trustworthy employees who would keep the business going in my absence—Herb was our financial expert and sales leader; Jane was the office manager and "Gal Friday"; Russ made sure that the orders were produced and shipped on time; and Elsie took care of the billing, correspondence, and work orders. All four contributed to a very well-run business—I couldn't have done it without them. They are all older than me and I gained so much from their experience.

I noticed at one particular Christmas party at the office that we had a healthy, international, and ecumenical group of employees. In the office was a gal from Paris, one from Germany, one from the Onondaga Indian Reservation, and one of Swedish nationality. In the warehouse, our work-leader and one other gal were African-Americans. Other employees were from Russia, Poland, Canada, and of course American-born. We had Jews, Catholics, Protestants, and Russian Orthodox all working together, young and old.

Generally, the Nagaragawa Hotel in Gifu was my base of operation. It was much easier to hold three meetings a day at one location and far more efficient. The Japanese were tremendous hosts but they wanted to monopolize your time so that you couldn't negotiate with other suppliers. If you went sight-seeing with them, your time with other suppliers was limited. Hotel rooms, train tickets, expensive meals, and gifts were all ploys to try to buy your business. I wanted five or six good suppliers, not one.

The production of cutlery was accomplished in the neighboring community of Seki, which was well known as the area that produced samurai swords hundreds of years before. A cottage industry is one where each component part is made in small factories then assembled in another. Each is relying on the other to be efficient so that all parts are completed on time. Having virtually no raw materials, Japan was dependant on cheap labor to be competitive with other countries. The balance of trade was out of kilter as they wanted to export completed goods but not import American-made products. The dollar vs. the yen was spiraling and goods from Japan were escalating in price every year. When we first bought products from Japan, the prices were very reasonable—most often far cheaper than goods produced here. But that changed over a twenty year period.

I made some good friends in the Orient, but friendship doesn't provide profit. It was time to move on to a more stable supplier system. I have written letters to my friends in Japan but since we no longer place orders there, they don't wish to correspond. They have been in my home and I have been welcomed into their homes as well. I feel sad that friendship with them is founded on business only. I hope to explore this issue and the war years with Japan in a follow-up book in the near future. That will be a lengthy book in itself.

We now bring in merchandise from Brazil and we haven't had a price increase in five years. The factory down there is huge—mostly on robotics. They can out-produce all the factories in Germany and Japan, combined, in any given day! It seems sad to think that we are one of only four knife companies still in existence in New York State when at one time New York was the, "cutlery capital."

The return stops in Hawaii were very welcome after all that negotiating. I have been very fortunate to visit Hawaii nine times since 1972. It is truly a PARADISE. I should be working for the Hawaii Tourist Board in their promotional department. I would be one of the best ambassadors they ever had.

Hawaii is called the "big island" with the city of Hilo on one side, and Kona on the other. Their coffee ranks in the top two in the world with that of Blue Mountain, Jamaica. Two of the largest volcanoes in the world are located here with one still active. You would associate cattle with Texas, but the largest cattle ranch in the U.S. is on this island. These ranches supply a great deal of the beef imported into Japan. They also supply the needs of Hawaii and the west coast of the U.S.

Kauai and Maui are much smaller but each has a different offering of beauty. You owe it to yourself to try the incredible seafood restaurants in the old whaling harbors. For one of the best dive or snorkel spots, try Black Rock near the Sheraton on Maui. The best prices on pineapples, washed sugar cane granules, coffee, and shirts is at the local Walmart, of all places. You can ship everything home at the UPS store in Kona.

Oahu probably has the most to offer of all the islands. You can enjoy the hustle and bustle of Honolulu and Waikiki or go over to the North shore for surfing and quaint little villages with authentic old Hawaii atmosphere. Ala Moana Mall is there for those who can't stay away from shopping or you can go to the flea market stalls of the International Market across from the hotels. Over near Diamond Head is one the best and safest places to snorkel at Hanama Bay—bring a lunch and spend the day. You can reach it by public transportation and equipment is for rent, very reasonably.

Don't forget Pearl Harbor. There is a movie at the museum which you should see prior to taking the launch out to the memorial. I hope that you're feeling my excitement! You owe it to yourself to go. Bring me with you; I'll be your tour guide!

I exhibited at trade shows in New York, Dallas, San Francisco, Orlando and St. Louis but I found Chicago to be the friendliest of all. There just is something to that mid-western hospitality—the people are so friendly. The shopping, museums, art galleries, and restaurants are not as numerous as New York but every bit as good.

The very first trade show I attended was at the Palmer House in Chicago. Our booth was on the 7th floor overlooking the indoor pool on the 6th. It made our display room very popular with the buyers because the flight crews stayed at the Palmer House and the flight attendants used the pool which you could see from our room. Just before the show opened we always seemed to be there for the St. Patrick's Day Parade which went by in front of the hotel.

One time I happened to find the door that led to the fire escape overlooking the street. While watching the parade, a young lady stepped out to watch also. We got to talking and she asked if I was staying at the hotel and inquired about the convention. The conversation turned to what she did and she explained that she was at the hotel for a promotional photography shoot. My assumption was that she was a model but I was told she was a Playboy "bunny".

I thought that I could have some fun with this. I told her that I was a member of the club and that I was taking customers out to dinner the next evening and could come by with them later. Would she pretend that she knew me and that we had gone out the night before? She agreed to this and let me know her name and what table to ask for when we got there. She went along with the whole charade as though we were dating.

Had they also been members, they would have known that "bunnies" were not allowed to date customers—but we had fun anyway.

The early clubs, as I remember, charged $1.00 for everything—a steak, a potato, a salad, glass of water, a pack of matches—you get the idea. So I really don't know if it was such a deal or not, but the club was a fun place to go to. Your membership was good at other clubs across the country. The Gaslight Club tried to compete but never really caught on.

Broadway shows came to Chicago but at a much lower ticket price. I remember seeing *"Hair"*, *"Oh Calcutta"*, and *"Chorus Line"*, to name a few. Seats were hard to come by especially if tickets weren't ordered in advance.

Our trade show quickly outgrew the Palmer House and moved over to Grant Park at the Hilton. We were there for maybe two more years until a permanent headquarters in Dallas was established.

The very first day in Dallas I had to see where President Kennedy was shot. People were coming there by the hundreds even in 1969. I walked up on the grassy knoll and could readily determine that the killing shot could easily have come from there. Press releases showed people turning their heads that way and one photo showed a puff of smoke in that direction. Today I wonder why the cover-up by the government? What difference does it make if there was one shooter or two? Why the big deal about a conspiracy?

There is no way that Lee Harvey Oswald could get that many shots off accurately at a target moving away from him. If it was a semi or fully-automatic then there's a remote possibility but a bolt action—no way—too much movement! I used to own the exact same model so I'm very familiar with the characteristics of the weapon. The lethal shot came from the front as indicated by the bone fragment and brain matter forensics and the movement of his head in the film of the event.

Just this week on television there was a show where four renowned scientists analyzed the evidence on the tapes and they all heard four shots, not three as per the Warren Commission Report. I've never, since the day of the assassination, believed in the lone gunman theory and you can't convince me otherwise.

Conventions-trade shows are designed for display of your product line, information on how to sell your products (case histories), dispensing catalogs, meeting new distributors and renewing old friendships. I would say that I've worked over 100 in my business career.

People are in too much of a hurry today. Distributors fly by your booth quickly handing out business cards to have you send them a catalog. Nobody takes the time to learn about your product line or how to sell it. When you combine the show with outside distractions such as water-theme parks, casinos, and resorts, the competition for their attention is worse. I'll take the old way!

Besides Chicago and Dallas I would select New York City for a convention location. Jacob Javits Convention Center or the Piers on the Hudson each offer a different venue for a trade show. It seems to be the business center of the world with Wall Street and so many large corporations based there.

When I go to Manhattan, I'm reminded of all the good times spent with family in earlier years. We'd stay at the Commodore near Grand Central but, as I recall, it was torn down a few years ago. I particularly like the St. Moritz on Central Park South for old world charm and central location. You're around the corner from Fifth Avenue shopping. Central Park is across the street, Rumplemeyer's (for breakfast) is on the ground floor, Harry's New York Bar is next door, Lincoln Center is just a short walk, and the Natural History Museum is a little bit farther on Central Park West. Also close by is the Russian Tea Room, Gallagher's Steak House on W. 52nd, the Palm Court at the Plaza, and Carnegie Hall.

Everyone traveling to New York should see the Empire State Building, the Statue of Liberty, Times Square and Broadway, South Street Seaport, Radio City Music Hall at Rockefeller Center, the new F.A.O. Schwartz toy store, and a carriage ride in Central Park. The city is full of excitement, at all hours.

I have enjoyed being a business man all these years and I'd still like to stay active in some way but my energy level isn't what it used to be. I now work at home and have no employees; and I still am self-employed after some 40 years. I can't get fired. I have no meetings to go to, no deadlines, and no commuting!

An accident in 1993 changed me physically, probably for the rest of my days. It really knocked the starch out of me and altered my lifestyle dramatically.

24

RAG DOLL

Since I was ten years old or so, I have been very interested in local history through the antique trade. I attended my first auction in Cazenovia as a youngster and I was hooked! Items were held up for all to see and usually a description followed as to the use and history (provenance). My parents were both avid auction-goers and it didn't take long for the bug to bite me.

Get to the auction site early to stake-out a seat near the front and take the time to slowly preview the merchandise that will shortly be put up for bid. Check everything carefully inspecting for chips, cracks, and most importantly—authenticity. There are a lot of repros and fakes out there so the "buyer beware!" Libraries have plenty of resources on antiques and there are some television shows that explain good antiques and their current value.

For a nine year period I became very active as a dealer exhibiting primitive furniture and kitchenware at small shows to begin with. Then after branching out to mall shows in other cities, I joined a co-op shop in Bouckville, NY where I had an awesome display of Empire and Victorian furniture and appropriate "smalls," as they're called. This allowed me to empty the truck at one location so I could be on the lookout for more deals "down the road."

My mom had a display in a different co-op specializing in what I called, "possibility furniture"—possibly someone would buy it! We were known by other dealers as "rough and ready." Along with the shows and the co-op location, I ran an old-fashion general store with authentic counters and displays. The store was stocked with grocery items not normally found locally. I sold gourmet coffees, pastas and sauces, rock candy, jams, jellies, candles, custom greeting cards and prints, hardware, furniture, and, of course, kitchen knives.

It was a fun project but considering the time spent, not too profitable—nothing ventured, nothing gained—as the expression goes.

At one point in time, I had the idea that my wares would fit in at the flea markets. There were numerous fairs and markets held throughout the state and these turned out to be quite profitable. They were usually a one or two day event which might mean a sleep-over at a local bed and breakfast. A 10'x 20' tent and some tables, a NYS tax form, and you were in business—as simple as that! I'd attend new merchandise auctions once or twice a week for back-up stock. Branching out to the eleven day NYS Fair was next and the granddaddy would be the Daytona Flea Market in Florida.

My son, Mike and I decided to make a two week jaunt into the South to get our feet wet in Volusia County, of all places. We first needed a permit to sell at the Market, as it is known, so a trip to the Volusia County Office was necessary. One look at my NYS driver's license started things off. We had to pay an out-of-state fee to sell down there and we were told that other fees might apply at the Market. At this point, we hadn't even set up yet and they had our Northern money already.

Daily we would move the truck to a different location at the Market so that the inspector couldn't see our New York plates—Yankee ingenuity!

I noticed that the KKK was alive and well in Volusia County as they had their own booth at the Daytona Flea Market where they were pitching for new members right out in the open! They had all sorts of merchandise for sale with KKK wording engraved or stamped on the items. Maybe if you joined, the stuff was free—like opening a charge account.

Showing curiosity, I stopped at the booth to ascertain the intelligence level of this individual. When I mentioned the words, Ku Klux Klan, he corrected me in that their version is targeted at Kikes, Koons, and Katholics. I chose not to get into it with him as my dad always cautioned me, "When arguing with an arrogant person, make sure he's not doing the same." I wonder if he had to pay a fee to sell his crap. Perhaps he got a *hate rate*!

The day before my 13th birthday, unknown to me, in a very small Southern town called Money, Mississippi, a boy only one year older than me was killed. You see he was a black boy who supposedly whistled at a pretty white woman. The boy's name was Emmett Till. He was in Money for a few days to visit his uncle, Moses Wright.

Emmett and other children went to Bryant's Grocery Store to get something cold to drink after picking cotton all day. The woman he was alleged to have whistled at was Bryant's wife, Carolyn. The anger in Roy Bryant got out of hand when about 2:30 AM, he and his half-brother (or brother-in-law—the stories differ) J.W. Milan, came to Moses' house. They took Emmett away under force and allegedly beat him, gouged out his eye, shot him in the head before lynching him with barbed-wire around his neck.

Mamie, Emmett's mom, came down from Chicago to bring her dead son's body home, back up North. Roy and J.W. were arrested on my birthday and indicted a few days later. In short, the jury deliberations took but 67 minutes with a "soda break" included. The two defendants were acquitted by 12 white males on September 23rd, the 166th anniversary of the Bill of Rights.

Mamie had the funeral home in Chicago view her son's body in an open casket just exactly as it was found in the river. A procession of 50,000 people filed by the casket. Included were the press from all over the world. A year later, J.W. admitted that he and Roy killed the boy. J.W. claimed that Emmett was insolent and defiant up to the end and never showed fear. *Look Magazine* covered the story.

Most people in the know claim that this case was foremost in the start of the Civil Rights Movement. The case had been reopened on May 10, 2004 and research indicates that as many as ten may have participated. J.W. died of cancer in 1980, Bryant died of cancer in 1990. Mamie died at age 81 on January 6, 2003.

"Strange Fruit" written by Abel Meeropol a.k.a. Lewis Allan goes like this:

> Southern trees bear strange fruit,
> Blood on the leaves and blood on the root,
> Black bodies swinging in the southern breeze,
> Strange fruit hanging from the poplar trees.
> Pastoral scene of the gallant South,
> The bulging eyes and the twisted mouth,
> Scent of magnolias, sweet and fresh,
> Then the sudden smell of burning flesh.
> Here is fruit for the crows to pluck,
> For the rain to gather, for the wind to suck,
> For the sun to rot, for the trees to drop,
> Here is a strange and bitter crop.

My very first exposure to the disease, AIDS, was at Bouckville when I met another antique dealer by the name of Bernie. He came to this country from Ireland. I believe it was at a time before the disease became epidemic across the world. I'm as guilty as others for not originally treating this disease seriously. The expressions going around at the time were, "Aids isn't all that bad—it turns fruits into vegetables," or "don't be gay, be happy." I'm embarrassed to have ever said that or to have felt that way toward another person. Only through education do you lose your ignorance!

Bernie had a male "friend" who was his business partner and companion. Bernie had AIDS and taught me a lot about antiques, and life as he experienced it. Bernie died after months of suffering and extreme weight loss. He was a Catholic and was concerned about his death in the eyes of the church, as a gay person. I'm positive that we have an understanding and compassionate Lord. I felt sorry for his friend who was experiencing a great loss in his life.

I have a lesbian friend also, but I won't use her name as she lives in the community. She revealed her life-style to me in confidence one day, over a beer. She was having problems with her girlfriend and, I guess, she felt that she could talk to me in private. I don't completely understand these relationships but I'm trying very hard not to be judgmental. As the lyrics in the Broadway play *"La Cage"* express, "I am what I am!" It's not a lifestyle for me but who am I to cast stones?

Getting to the point of the story, it appears in the paper that a good auction is coming up and I called Mom to see if she wanted to go with me. As fate would have it, we decided on taking two cars just in case one of us wants to leave early—lucky her! She is probably two blocks ahead of me in her car as we're coming into a nearby town where the auction is to be held.

I'm approaching what is called the "hump" bridge which goes over the railroad tracks. You can't see the road on the other side but I can hear a car coming and the screeching of tires tells me it is moving pretty fast. As I later found out from the police, the driver is a 17 year old girl who has only had her license for one week. It turns out that the girl's mother had been in an accident in East Syracuse and she was on the way to the hospital to see her. With the rush of adrenalin and driver inexperience, she was, according to several witnesses, traveling at 60–65 mph. in a 30 zone. She had already swerved around two cars and just narrowly missed running over six joggers along the side of the road.

Over the bridge and slightly airborne the car bounces off the guardrail and is now headed right at me. I'm doing exactly 30mph, but I'm in a big Isuzu truck. There's an instant look of sheer terror on her face seconds before impact. I don't have time to avoid her because I didn't see her until it was too late.

Her car impacts the truck on the left front panel and tire, just below the driver's door. She glances off the big **Yokohama** tire, wipes out and explodes both tandem batteries underneath the truck body, eliminates the catalytic converter and exhaust system before hitting the rear tandem tires where her car ends up in the middle of the road. The car is crushed and I'm later told that it takes a great deal of time to cut away the top and doors to get to her.

Weeks later my lawyer had to go to Angela's house to serve papers on an insurance claim as she was ticketed for numerous infractions and was considered "at fault." In her house was a picture of her prior to the accident. This young gal suffered broken arms, legs, ribs, and a badly cut face, according to my attorney. A fraction of a second can change your whole life.

The impact made me grip the steering wheel tighter while my body was thrown like a rag doll inside the cab. I couldn't feel my fingers for several days as my hands and arms experienced trauma from losing my grip. My legs were caught in the area near the pedals while my upper body was thrown over the center shift into the passenger seat.

Two things contributed to this—not wearing a seat belt and a trucker's beaded back rest which acted like ball bearings. I remember my head whipping back and forth and it became wedged between the two seats.

The fire department responded very rapidly to both of us. I was transported to the hospital on a backboard and laid there for nearly two hours before anyone paid attention to me. The x-rays were misread and I was discharged with a broken neck which my seven year old daughter saw on the films, several days later. An orthopedic doctor came up with the same conclusion after reading the x-rays in his office. My own insurance company was released and didn't have to settle based on the fact that a seat belt wasn't used. I can't argue that; and I'm very thankful that I wasn't hurt worse.

Many years of physical and massage therapy has helped but it doesn't really take the pain away. Life is like a card game. Poker Annie would say, "you play the cards you're dealt."

There was a point in my life years ago that I thought **Jack Daniels** was a good pain killer for neck problems but all it did was create new ailments. When I quit drinking six years ago, I'll bet **Jack Daniels** stock dropped three points on the NYSE!

The surgeon told me that I would probably have arthritis as a result of the accident and was he ever correct—the pain and swelling is with me constantly! I could be a weatherman as my fingers can sense the slightest change in barometric pressure and now I'm always a "pain in the neck," among other places!

These health issues to me are like "speed bumps," something else to slow you down!

25

DIB

He was the youngest of the children in his family and seemed to be mothered by his sisters throughout his whole life. They influenced just about every aspect of his life with un-requested opinions on ours, as well. Friction was always there when they were near me or my mom.

Dib, my dad, must have been smart in school for I believe he skipped two grades. Going to a one room schoolhouse gave him the advantage of listening to older student's lessons.

I know that he was an athlete as I've seen early pictures of him in uniforms playing basketball and football. He worked after school as, what they called, a "soda jerk" in a drug store in Jordan, NY. He graduated early and started working for the Lighting Company (now Niagara Mohawk-National Grid) in Syracuse. During the war years he worked for General Electric at Carrier Circle doing time and efficiency studies. G.E. made electric turbines for the U.S. Navy and this facility also served as a training base for that equipment.

He had quite a love for preserving the past and that's why I think he liked history so much. We would take trips to Gettysburg, Yorktown, Charleston, Williamsburg, Plymouth, and Washington, D.C. to get filled up on famous battle sites and historical information. He had a very good grasp of American history.

I have fond memories of road trips out in the country listening to his "down home" tales and particularly, his songs.

You've probably already deduced that he and I didn't get along. How would you like to be told by your father that he wished you were never born? What could I have possibly done or said to bring out that kind of feeling? At least I knew where I stood!

After his funeral his new wife informed me that she was sure that he loved me. It would have been nice to hear that once from him, directly. I guess you could say that during our lifetime I loved him, but didn't like him. As I told you before, I lost respect for him and really disliked the way he treated my mother.

There are other things that I know about him that aren't going to be printed here. My brother and sisters had a different relationship with him and it's proper that their memories of him are not disturbed. Besides, it isn't going to change anything and they probably wouldn't believe me anyway.

I came to visit him in the hospital after he suffered a heart attack. He was moved eventually to a regular care unit from ICU as his progress was steady. A trip was planned to Disney World with all the children for a week. I told him that we could postpone but he said that he was getting stronger and not to worry. "Go ahead," he said.

We went ahead with our plans, as he insisted. On return to our hotel room after a birthday celebration at Disney for our daughter, Kathy, the flashing light on the phone gave me an indication that all was not right. He died at age 68 in January of 1980.

We flew home the following day to be joined by others for a very peculiar funeral. His new wife had her attorney show up at the funeral home to let us know that we were not included in his will. This, I'm sure, made her feel good. These procedures are normally handled weeks, sometimes months, later. The will would have been contested had I known all the circumstances at the time, but it won't change anything either. I now know why she wanted it expedited.

We had a funeral mass downtown at the Cathedral, with no casket! She wouldn't allow for this—never knew why. Did you ever go to a funeral and the deceased wasn't present? The parish priest thought it was most bizarre. He wasn't cremated; she just didn't want a church service for some reason.

I hope that you've read enough because I sure am tired of this subject. It was part of my life and I cried at his wake wishing that we could have had a better relationship. If you're in the same boat, patch things up before you sink!

Life is far too short. Don't take it seriously—you won't get out of it alive anyway! If you still have a dad, hug him for me and let him know how much you love him before it is too late.

Go see him or call him!

26

HAVING FUN

"You can't add years to your life, but you can add life to your years!"

When you work hard, balance that with playing hard. *"Take time to smell the roses,"* they say. Develop some outside interests.

Growing up on water most of my life, boating, water skiing, and fishing took up a good deal of my time. In the winter I could then switch over to downhill or cross-country skiing with no problem. In this area, with such long winters, it is best to keep active.

With the bagpipe band, we would practice our music in the winter and participate in parades and competitions in the spring and summer. The three oldest boys, Robert, Mike, and John were in the band with me so it gave me the opportunity to be with them more often. I was very proud when Mike won the North American Trophy in Kingston, Ontario at age 12, beating out guys much older than him in high school and college. We all played for three years with Syracuse Scottish and then my son, John and I played for another two years with the 78th Fraser Highlanders out of Rome, NY.

I wish now though that there was a similar activity for my daughters. I sometimes felt that they were short-changed.

I like to read all types of books and very seldom watch television unless it's an educational channel like Nova, Nature on Public TV, Discovery Channel, National Geographic, History Channel, Travel, Antique Road Show, or Jacques Cousteau. Game shows and situation comedies, with canned laughter, don't hold my interest. They have shows that air as reality shows but really couldn't be farther from the truth. My take on television of today is, "garbage in, garbage out." I'm not a big fan of pro sports but I do watch lacrosse, figure skating competitions, and the Olympics.

Lacrosse is undoubtedly my favorite so I'd like to let my family know now that two lacrosse sticks and a ball in my casket would be appropriate, just in case someone in the "next world" wants to play catch. I'll go anywhere to see a good game. I follow Syracuse University gals and guys home games and have traveled to a few away ones also.

I work in the penalty box at the Tsha' Hon'nonyen'dakhwa'("where they play games") on the Onondaga Nation Territory for the indoor box lacrosse seasons. Central NY is where the game started called Dehontshihgwa-ehs (the Creator's game). Canadians will tell you otherwise; but they learned about it from the many trips the Jesuits made to this territory trying to convert the Haudenosaunee (Iroquois) to Catholicism.

The Five Nations (Mohawk, Oneida, Onondaga, Cayuga, and Seneca) later joined by the Tuscarora, played the game for hundreds of years. I hope that you're interested enough to read a follow-up book on Northeastern tribes that I'll be writing after this one. It will be Part II of a trilogy I'm developing.

My interest in Native Americans continues to this day by attending local pow-wows, craft fairs, and gatherings at the NYS Fair. The largest gathering that I have ever attended was at Foxwoods Casino in Connecticut. It is held every August and is called the *Schemitzun*. There were 21 drum bands, with 550 tribes represented from all over the states, Canada, Mexico, and Central America. They also put on a Native American rodeo. You can purchase Native American food of buffalo, caribou, elk, venison, tacos, fry bread, etc. They have clothing, jewelry, crafts, prints, and paintings for sale. There must have been at least 3,000 dancers inside a tent the size of four football fields, to give you some perspective. It was a three day event and I was there every minute!

My wife is the commuter in the family, so most generally I do the cooking so that the meal is ready when she gets home. I really enjoy making soups from scratch—they usually turn out pretty good. Emeril Live has some good ideas and recipes—BAM—another notch—anything to change my cooking from ordinary meat and potatoes. Rachael Ray of the Food Network is now on the rise with her famous 30 minute meals. Weekends are taken over by Michelle with her gourmet 20 minute meals—delicious! Speaking of Michelle, I want you to know that I met her at the post office. You might say that, *"I went in for the mail and ended up with a female."*

Carrying forward the family tradition, I raise bees in our backyard. I'm not sure if the neighbors know yet, but they will if they read this. It is truly fascinating to watch them go about their business (the bees, not the neighbors). The queen is capable of laying 1,000 to 3,000 eggs per week if the conditions are right. The mature bees fly out in a two mile radius of the hive to gather pollen and nectar. We had some honey this year and it's really delicious. The honey is good for allergies and it's reported that bee stings contain a beta-blocker to suppress arthritis pain. The honey itself is a natural sugar and has positive qualities for your whole body. You've never seen a bee in the hospital, now have you?

When my daughters' friends come over to visit, I let them know in advance that we have them in our backyard and that they are friendly. I give them permission to "pet" them if they'd like to, but I have had no takers, as of now.

Vegetable gardening was a favorite hobby of mine until arthritis kept me from taking care of the plants the way I should. Now a small patch serves the need to grow something of my own—a hobby learned from my dad. I have fruit trees, a berry patch, and grapevines, as well, which keep me occupied.

NASCAR is probably the fastest growing sport in the United States. For the past few years I have been able to see it live at Watkins Glen which is about 1 ½ hours from our house. I try to get a pit row seat which gives you a great view of turns 1 and 2 and the lower part of 3 as it goes up the hill. Right below my seat is where the cars come in to pit for tires, fuel, or car adjustments. This course separates the men from the boys as the track is unforgiving to the standard oval driver. There are right and left turns, uphill climbs and gravity defying down runs. Without the "boot," the course measures approximately 2 ½ miles.

NASCAR seems to be a beer crowd while Formula One has a champagne taste—totally different crowd. Formula One is coming back to the Glen in September.

A pit row ticket allows you to see the time trials on Thursday and Friday as well as the Busch Race on Saturday. Early on Sunday morning, as long as you're wearing appropriate clothing (long pants and shirts because of the fuel) and you have a pit row pass, you can walk along near the cars and crews, up close.

Minutes before the race was to start, they send a car out to "clear the track." It really isn't necessary anymore because each sector has "spotters." They call in information on their particular zone to the tower. But I guess for tradition they still do it.

ESPN was covering the race that year and I was wearing a CBS cap that my son, Robert, had given me. The official must have thought that I might be there to check out the event for future broadcasts. I didn't confirm, nor deny. He asked if I was interested in riding with him. How fast can you say "Yes?" I'm riding "shotgun" in the front seat and I am told to pull the seatbelt strap as tight as I can. Next question, "How fast do you want to go?" You can guess my response.

I had been on that track several years before with my mom's Mercedes 190SL going well over 100. He beat that easily—they now travel at speeds exceeding 200mph. My heart is now much older than it was then in the 60s. The thrill, with him driving, was much more intense. We went around that track in a blur. What a day, and it was just beginning.

The track image has changed dramatically in that the "bog" has been filled in where they used to conduct topless dirt bike jumping contests for the girls. Spectators enjoyed this almost as much as the race. Gone are the military encampments on the knoll at turn #1. Tents, half-tracks, Jeeps, howitzers, and 'Nam vets staked out this area as their own! Now it's bleachers and high-priced tickets.

Jeff Gordon and Dale Earnhardt Sr. are in pit positions #1 and #2—right in front of my seat. A beautiful August afternoon in New York—the sun is hot, the beer is cold! This is what I call HAVING FUN. I wish that I could share this with Michelle but she's probably at home by the pool with a good book, having fun in her own way.

After the race is over you might as well be prepared for a very long wait. It's not exactly a super highway into town—just a two lane country road to handle 250,000 people! I know of a restaurant out of town on the way to Geneva where the drivers used to catch dinner before leaving the area. Jackie Stewart, Sterling Moss and others used to eat there in the days before Bud at the Glen, when Formula One was king.

Any way, that's where I'm headed to eat before the crowd gets there. Drivers and crews used to come in by helicopter to avoid the traffic.

After dinner, while paying my bill at the counter, who walks up but Dale Earnhardt. While waiting for his wife, who has gone to the ladies room, I was reminiscing with him about the 30–35 years I've been coming to the track for different race events and what races were like years ago. I had read a recent article about his philanthropy to charity causes and I let him know what a good thing he was doing. He asked if I wanted his autograph (I know I'm going to annoy certain readers), but I told him that I didn't place importance on collecting signatures. He obviously was not familiar with that type of response. I had better stop meeting famous people because he and Martin Luther King both died two years after I met them.

In my younger days, pre-broken neck, a new dance came along every month. I was just getting the hang of one when a new one appeared on the scene. See if I've left out any from your memory—boogaloo, shing-a-ling, watusi, twist, dog, swim, stroll, bump, jerk, monkey, frug, slop, bosa nova, bop, peppermint twist, funky chicken, slide, huckleback, hand jive, madison, locomotion, fly, limbo rock, shimmy, and the mashed potato. If I've omitted any, let me know.

Solo dancing was starting and a dancer's loyalty was no longer to the partner but to the group. On Saturdays we all watched the kids in Philadelphia on Dick Clark's *American Bandstand* which started on July 9, 1956.

In 1954 Texas Instruments pioneered the portable transistor radio making it possible to bring your music with you to school, the beach, and most importantly, away from parental criticism.

"Having fun," for me, also involves concerts, ethnic fairs, attending the NY State Fair, auctions, antique shows, Syracuse U. football and lacrosse games, and Broadway plays that tour our city. I'm also content just to go for a walk in the neighborhood with my wife.

Since I'm no longer able to participate in sports, I'm the most loyal spectator at our local high school, Fayetteville-Manlius. I'm on the eleven member Sports Advisory Council with our athletic director. It gives me a chance to get involved, to contribute! We are a small, centralized school district with a big heart.

I love to brag, so I'll let you know we are #1 this year in the entire state in six categories—boy's cross country, girl's lacrosse, girl's tennis (210 straight matches over nine years), boy's soccer, girl's novice crew, and boy's novice crew. In addition to being #1 state-ranked in cross country, they are #1 in the nation! I truly enjoy high school sports whether or not I have a son or daughter playing. I might add that the girl's volleyball and tennis teams invited me to their team banquets this year—great company, great food!

I might add that we finished #1 in the nation in the National Science Olympics, also.

The international group, "Up with People," was coming to put on performances in August of 2000 at our high school. I thought having students from foreign countries would be a good learning experience for our children. They were looking for host families to house, feed, and transport some 150 kids of high school and college age. Normally they would place one child per family, but pickings were slim. We signed up for four girls—we ended up with ten!

They all came in one evening by motor coaches to our Senior Center in Manlius. After meeting them all, we had to make several trips to our house with singers, dancers, and suitcases. Grace before the meal was said that night in Norwegian, the following night in Japanese. With our family and ten foreign students, we had a house full. I never knew girls could eat so much! Against the rules, they were up late at our house enjoying the pool, hot tub, and sauna (I think a few beers also). They had been traveling all day and this relaxing was "just what the doctor ordered," as the expression goes.

Early morning found the girls from Holland and Norway out for a run in the neighborhood with our daughter, Mackenzie. You already know how I love breakfast and so do young girls from all over the world. Thank God we had two showers and multiple hair dryers. Getting two off to school in the morning is bad enough, but ten at the same time to rehearsals was interesting, to say the least. We were parents to these girls for three days and two nights. Being a parent/host, I was able to see a morning rehearsal before I rushed to get our ten lovely ladies some sandwiches, chips, cookies, and drinks for lunch.

We all had front-row seats that night for an incredible show that had a theme about overcoming prejudice and working toward world peace. These kids had auditioned for these parts and I would proclaim that they were every bit as good as a Broadway company.

The word had spread about our backyard as more cast members and staff joined us in the evening at a bonfire by the pool. Some never got to sleep until early in the morning. They had to leave the following morning of the third day to catch a plane to Italy. They were going to perform in front of the Pope at the Vatican for the *"Year of the Child"* celebration. We were able to see part of it on television.

I today, feel very sad for them because none of us knew that was to be their last performance. Up with People, based in the United States, was closing down due to financial difficulties. They were one of five casts traveling around the world that had to be notified to return to their homes as best they could. I tried to keep up the e-mails and correspondence but life moves on. The days go by but the memories linger. I hope that their message got out to the world—Lord knows we need it!

27

STRANGE HAPPENINGS

Four things have happened to me that I can't explain and, quite possibly, nobody can. I am a well-educated person and I'm prone to be a realist. I don't believe in the occult, the supernatural, or superstitions. I guess that I need to see or experience something for myself rather than taking a person's word as fact. I don't necessarily doubt a situation but I would like to verify the evidence myself.

In the later years of high school and through college, during conversations with people, I was able to finish an individual's sentence. Quite often these were complete strangers that I had never before spoken with and would have no advanced knowledge of their experiences or thought patterns. They would look at me in amazement that I could blurt out words to finish what they had to say. This only lasted a few years and never has returned.

Mom was getting along in age and expressed a particular interest in going to Honesdale, Pennsylvania to show me where her dad grew up after moving from Manhattan. Every year when she was young, they would travel to Honesdale to place flowers on the graves on Memorial Day.

After having lunch in town, she told me how to get to the house where her dad lived with his family. It was just out of town, up on a hill in the country. She still remembered exactly how to find it after all those years of being away.

As we're approaching the farm house, perhaps 40 to 50 yards away, she said, "Oh, look Jack, there's Grandpa on the porch waving to us." Instinctively I looked to where she was pointing.

The porch went across the front of the house and in the middle were two steps down to the lawn. Just above the top step stood a man in an all-white suit—jacket, slacks, vest, and tie. He was holding a white hat in one hand a waving to us with the other. She didn't wave back but turned to me in the seat with a really puzzled look on her face. We both instantly looked back again and the image (I use that word from lack of understanding of what we saw), was gone. I stopped the car so that two grown adults could compare notes on what we had just experienced. We saw exactly the same thing at the same time and there wasn't any way to explain it. I was not going to walk up to that house. He had died many, many years ago.

She had seen John Burns, her grandfather, and I had just seen my great-grandfather! No, we had not had a liquid lunch, but I'm sure we could have used a drink after that. Mom and I talked about it over the years. It's one of those happenings where you had to be there to appreciate what transpired.

My sister-in-law, Judy, lost her brother Nick when he was about 19 years old. He died from a disease that affects Italians particularly if both parents are of Italian descent. She and her sister, Paula, were the only two children left. Paula was a really nice gal and always seemed to have a bright outlook on life even though this disease was always hanging around to remind her of mortality. She didn't dwell on it.

Paula died a few years ago, long before her time. It was very hard on the parents, and particularly on Judy. During the night, a few days after the funeral, Paula came to give me a message. I awoke from a sound sleep with a feeling that someone was in our bedroom. My wife continued to sleep through the night and she wasn't aware of this appearance until I told her in the morning.

Paula was at the foot of the bed giving me instructions to let Judy know that she was fine. "What do you mean? You're dead!" I said. Paula's response: "I know that! Now will you just do what I'm asking? Just let her know that I'm okay."

The image disappeared as quickly as it had arrived but I was awake the rest of the night. The following day I called Judy to let her know about this "conversation." She has never to this day talked about it. She either accepts it or thinks that her brother-in-law is a little "touched."

A few years ago I was experiencing some stomach trouble and a gastrointestinal doctor was consulted. He scheduled me for both a lower and upper G.I. series at the hospital. They told Michelle that both procedures would take some time so there was no point in her waiting. She could go to work and a nurse would call her later to pick me up.

I was given an injection just after, "I signed my life away." Off to sleep I went while they started to check out where processed food goes. Next, came the upper part. I don't want to scare you with the details—you may need it some day, so ignore me. I'm rudely awakened by slaps on my face and two nurses yelling in my ear to "wake up and come out of it!"

Prior to this I'm going down a brightly lit tunnel. Everything is peaceful-no pain, no sound. At the end of the tunnel the light is more intense than the sun but I don't have to squint and there's, again, no pain. I'm told later by the head nurse that my breathing had stopped and that they were afraid of "losing" me.

If where I'm to ultimately go is anything like what I experienced, then I can tell you it is most peaceful and serene. I'm not in a hurry to see where the tunnel leads—I'm not that curious!

I do know that wherever I go, I'll have friends. This narrative does not carry a "certificate of authenticity"—you'll just have to trust me!

28

MOM

I've told you a great deal about her already but later on in life she had some health issues that changed the quality of her life. My mom had open heart surgery a few years before. She had a leaking heart valve that was replaced by a mitral pig valve. She was a good sport about it because the "pig jokes" kept coming. She couldn't "root" for Syracuse any longer as she was now an Arkansas Razorback fan. She could no longer eat her relatives—bacon, ham, etc. Her relatives would be kicked around during football season. Her kitchen table was no longer needed—any old trough would do. You get the idea.

This valve gave her a little more time. She was a fighter that really loved life. She looked forward to each new day and new experiences. She met new friends each day. They were the same people but when you have Alzheimer's, they're new each day.

She'd come up to our house nearly every Sunday for a family dinner. Michelle's parents were nice enough to pick her up on the way. It was a means of keeping in touch and a way to be sure that she was eating properly. Her loss of appetite wasn't helping in attempts to keep her strong. We bought a meal supplement product called **Ensure** but she wouldn't drink it.

The decision was made to move her to a facility near our house which had assisted living arrangements. She had her own small apartment—a bedroom, bathroom with a shower, a living room, and an eating area which wasn't really needed. They provided three full, hot meals each day with cookies, snacks, coffee, and tea all day. They changed your linen, and cleaned your room on a weekly basis.

Down the hall was a large common area for mini-concerts, meetings, or "happy hours" before dinner. They need to change the wording as nobody seems to be happy to be there. She often threatened to catch the Greyhound out front and beat it to Florida. Knowing her as I did, it wouldn't have surprised me!

Her close friends weren't coming to see her but I couldn't bear to tell her that they were dying or that they too were sick and needed attention at their own place of rest. She put up with craft projects and bingo games just to appease me. I knew she wasn't happy, but we were all running out of options.

Mom couldn't live alone anymore, or keep her car. She had been in two minor accidents, both of which were probably her fault. Joan and her husband Jim, who live in Rochester, would come to see her every month. It was Jim's job to decorate her apartment door with each new season which helped her to keep in touch with the outside world.

We all noticed that her trips to the liquor store were more frequent in direct proportion to her depression and pain. I felt that in her late 80s what's the point in denying her one more thing? We had taken away everything else.

Sometimes she would take the Wynwood shuttle over to our church, sometimes she'd go with us. This particular Sunday morning we picked her up for mass. During Fr. Sestito's sermon it seemed that she had just rested her head on Michelle's shoulder and fallen asleep.

A young gal by the name of Lisa is a member of our parish and as it turned out is an RN. She teaches other nurses and doctors the art of CPR. She and her daughter, Rachel, were usually on the look-out for Mom as there's one part in mass where everyone shakes hands and gives a greeting of peace. Rachel liked my mom and looked forward to this part of the service—Thank God!

Within seconds Lisa was at Mom's side taking vital signs—there weren't any! Four doctors and two other nurses apparently go to the 10:30 mass and were in the aisle in seconds helping Lisa to lay her on the floor and start CPR while the ambulance was on the way. I guess the good Lord didn't want her just then for it was two more years before the fatal one would hit while she was in a nursing home. I'm tearing-up while I'm typing this—I miss her so much. I thank Lisa and Rachel for that extra time they gave her.

Michelle and I went over to see her after work one evening and the nurse took us aside to tell us that she didn't have a good day. I tried to keep the conversation light because we could see that she was in pain and quite thirsty, for the doctor had given orders for "nothing by mouth."

I had to get home to have supper ready for our teenagers, but I told her that I'd be back after dinner and we could talk some more. She whispered to me to bring her a little Irish whiskey because she was thirsty and I told her that I'd see what I could do. Those were her last words to me. Even at the end she maintained her Irish wit and could come up with something to put me at ease. That was her way, she never focused on herself.

Michelle stayed for another hour while I went home. The girls were home from school and I don't like to leave them home alone. We talked after dinner as to whether she would make it through the night but a phone call from Loretto confirmed our worst fears. As before, Michelle was the last to be there for her.

I can't say enough about pre-planning a funeral. Joan, Jim, Michelle, and I had discussed arrangements weeks before. The funeral director knew exactly what our wishes were for our mom.

Jim Clough showed up with the 78th Fraser Pipe Band and my boys were on the drums. It takes a good Scottish pipe band to send off a good Irish lady. St. Peter had early warning that she was on her way! Jim asked me if the priest would mind if they opened the drones all the way (allowing for big sound). I figured Father Kevin wouldn't care, so she came into church in style. As in the song, *Danny Boy*, "the pipes are calling."

When her casket was placed in the ground next to her parents, the St. Patrick's Day parade started in downtown Syracuse. I thought that it was nice of them to wait for her.

My daughter, Jacki, and her family hosted an old-fashioned Irish hooley at their home until the wee hours—lots of food, lots of singing, lots of beer, and lots of Irish whiskey. We left an **Old Bushmills** in her casket so she won't be thirsty again! The next time that I see her though, I'm going to hear about it—I didn't take the cap off!

She always talked about the cherry blossoms in Washington after returning from her trips to see Bill at Georgetown or Joan and Linda at Catholic University. We got permission to plant a cherry tree outside the window of the apartment where she used to live, hoping that it will brighten up the day of someone else.

One of the doctors in the church during her heart attack was an optometrist. Days later after her heart attack, she couldn't let that go by without a comment that he was the only one that could "see" that she was in trouble. She asked me if she had halted Fr. Sestito's sermon. I said that she did—a smile came on her face!

She once told me that people pass on to make room in this world for the newborn. She had told me earlier in the hospital that her time was coming so there'd be room for Mike and Staci's son, Cole, her great-grandson.

She was one of my best friends and I'm really glad that I had the chance to know her so well. It's nice to be able to talk with someone without them being so opinionated—I'll have to work on that! She is truly missed.

Not known to anyone until this writing is the fact that she donated a considerable amount of money many years ago that would enable Lemoyne College to construct their first building on campus. This donation was to be anonymous but I thought you'd like to know about her generosity.

29

TWIN TERROR—MURDER IN THE MORNING

I can vividly recall where I was that morning—watching Good Morning America (what a name for a show, on that day) when our lives changed forever at 8:46a.m.

On September 11, 2001, I was out in the kitchen getting a second cup of coffee as an image of a plane crashing into the Twin Towers of the World Trade Center was on television when I returned to the bedroom.

My first reaction was that they were previewing a new movie coming out and this was a clip from that. But the reporters were slowly putting pieces of this happening together. I quickly switched to the other stations for a reality check. All were starting to get the same information but with slightly different camera coverage.

According to the BBC report I have, the FAA alerted NORAD at 8:38 a.m. that American Airlines Flight 11 had been hijacked. It hit the North Tower at 8:46a.m. At 8:53, F-15 fighters are scrambled from Otis AFB in Falmouth, MA. At 9:03a.m. FAA notifies NORAD that United 175 has been hijacked. United Airlines Flight 175 hits the South Tower at 9:03. At 9:37, American Airlines Flight 77 crashed into the Pentagon in Washington. At 10:03a.m. United Airlines Flight 93 crashed into the ground 80 miles southeast of Pittsburgh. (BBC News-Timeline-bbc.co.uk America's Day of Terror)

Sometime during all of this, and I never thought to check my watch, F-16s took off from the 174th Fighter Wing of the NY Air National Guard at Hancock Air Base here in Syracuse and going like a "bat out of hell," nearly took the top off our chimney. Our house sits high on a hill southeast of the airbase about ten miles away. Their initial heading would take them towards NYC. They were on a flight pattern I had never observed before. You could just sense by the way they flew that they were on a serious mission and meant business.

I was glued to the television screen just as I was for John F. Kennedy, Robert Kennedy, and Martin Luther King's funerals.

It didn't seem real. It's as though you were looking at a prime time movie. My son, Chris, had been on the phone with a former classmate from college. That fellow was going down to the main floor to meet another friend at the coffee shop when the first plane hit. They, by fate, were safe.

I don't think that we have been attacked on our mainland since the War of 1812. The Japanese bombed Pearl Harbor and invaded the Aleutian Islands in WW II but Hawaii and Alaska were not states at the time. Hitler was plotting with the Mexicans to invade us during WW II, but it never happened.

The singer, Linda Eder, has a compact disc out called *"GOLD."* Listen with some Kleenex to song # 14, *"If I had My Way."* It sums up my feelings on post-9/11. She has other songs about relationships that are equally as good. Yes, I cry. It might surprise you, but men are emotional, too.

W.P. Shealy Company
506 W. Adams St.
P.O. Box 2008
Dothan, AL 36302

9/20/01

Jack Edgerton
The General Store, Inc.
Jack:
Enclosed you will find the two Bar B Que sets you were kind enough to send down here for us to show a customer. Unfortunately they chose a couple of other items. I appreciate your help and support of our sales effort.

Mr. Shealy had a good time talking to you the other day. He is my Father-in-Law and he thinks a lot of you. He said your group had a good time on the trip over to Hawaii. I hope to go there one day but, I have to get two boys through college first. Once again thank you for rushing these out for us. It is nice to enjoy that kind of support from such a fine supplier as you.

Sincerely,

Gene Martin

PS I do not know where your home town is in relation to the WTC area. I want you to know that last Tuesday I was in Prattville, Alabama just ready to go out and make calls when I saw the tragic events unfold. I can honestly say that there are not words enough to express the feelings that we all feel down here for you fine folks in New York. There are not any northern Americans, southern Americans, white Americans or black Americans anymore. We are all just Americans facing some people that hate us with a venom that is hard to comprehend. Our heart felt prayers go out to all of New York during this time.

There isn't really a great deal more that I could write about my life from my personal memory and recollections that is important enough. There are minor episodes but I won't bore you anymore. I have health issues as I'm sure anyone my age does, but we're not going to get into that here. Suffice it to say, that from head (thinning hair) to toe (arthritis/gout), I could use some new body parts. That's what is expressed every year to my wife and kids when in their frustration, they ask, "What do you want for Christmas?"

I want to think about what I can do, rather than what I can't. Years ago when I heard about someone's ailments, I would say, "It could have been worse—it could have been me!" I try not to use that expression now—I don't find it funny anymore. When you get older you get closer to God (both ways). With my meter running down," I'm looking for people with extra quarters."

Age is an issue of mind over matter…if you don't mind, it doesn't matter!

At age   4, success is…not peeing in your pants.
At age 12, success is…having friends.
At age 16, success is…having a driver's license.
At age 35, success is…having money.
At age 50, success is…having money.
At age 70, success is…having a driver's license.
At age 75, success is…having friends.
At age 80, success is…not peeing in your pants.

When I put money in the collection box on Sunday, I no longer consider it as donating but more as investing. But, I'm really not worried, for you see wherever I go, I'll have friends!

I was born in 1943 so let's look at the good and the bad of that time. We are the 'baby boomers,' those of age 44 to 62 years of age.

"We are called the 'Woodstock Generation.' Even those who weren't hippies shared the idealism and optimism of the late 60s and early 70s. The 'Me Generation' as we're also called, is supposed to be the most spoiled and self-indulgent age bracket in U.S. history. We are the result of child-focused parents.

We were the largest generation in history with unprecedented prosperity and parental indulgence. We were relatively free from financial fears. We were the TV generation with our own music and heroes." (PPB magazine November 2004 pg. 85–86)

II
EVERTHING IS "SWELL"
1943

30

THE HOMEFRONT

Being a youngster during the war, I remember staring out the window watching trains go by carrying troops and weapons to the docks in New York and New Jersey and watching bomber groups form up over our house as they took off from the airport. Dib said they were headed to Newfoundland, wherever that was.

"Syracuse Bomber Hops Channel, Hit 200 Times"

"A Flying Fortress, *'Boom Town'*, which once attracted the gaze of all Syracuse and Central New York as it roared thru the skyways in formation practice flights to and from Syracuse army air base, is now a wrecked ship, (with) 200 anti-aircraft shell and machine gun bullets in her steel hide, somewhere in England.

One of her crew is dead. The other nine, including the husband of a Syracuse woman, are back on the job, now manning another Flying Fortress, *'Boom Town Junior'* unloading their cargoes of death and destruction on the Nazi-held European continent. The story of *'Boom Town'* and her youthful crew who roamed the streets of Syracuse only six months ago is told by her pilot, Capt. Clyde B. Walker of Oklahoma, in a story wired from London. It is told in *The American Magazine* this month.

The ship's crew, besides the pilot was Lt. William J. Reed, co-pilot; Lt. W.M. Smith, navigator; Lt. Grover Cleveland Bentinck, bombardier; Sgt. Stephen Krucher, tail gunner; Sgt. Oscar R. Green, ball turret gunner; Staff Sgt. Louis P. Berring (my wife's uncle) right waist gunner; Sgt. William M. Stroud, waist gunner; Sgt. Philip L. Judkins, top turret gunner, and John T. Frisholz, radio operator.

No word of the death flight or the seven preceding raids of *'Boom Town'* was ever written in the many letters received here by the bride of Sgt. Berring, who pumped round after round of machine gun slugs into the Luftwaffe wolves.

Sgt. Berring, and his bride, Mrs. Ruth Avery Berring, 128 Hixson Ave., were married last September in St. Joseph's (French) Church shortly before *'Boom Town'* took off from the Syracuse air base for the last time.

A moment after *'Boom Town'* dropped her bombs on the L'orient sub base, the bombardier, Lt. Bentinck of Galveston, Tex., jubilantly shouted 'bull's eye!' Those were his last words.

A storm of anti-aircraft shells burst all about the ship and a flock of wolves emptied their 20 mm cannon and machine gun bullets into 'Boom Town.' The anti-aircraft 'flak' finished Lt. Bentinck instantly. The navigator was wounded and knocked unconscious. The ship was ripped and wracked in every quarter. The radio operator was wounded. Flames burst forth in the radio room.

'Boom Town' nosed down for shelter in the clouds, but kept on fighting and accounted for the end of three of the wolves, and two more 'probables.' *'Boom Town'* staggered over the water toward England, losing altitude all the way, bouncing down onto the waves and bounding up again for the rest of her 100 mile journey. In a last heroic effort *'Boom Town'* cleared the cliffs of Dover and limped on to a nearby field. *'Boom Town'* landed safely, but for the last time."

—(*The Post Standard*-Friday, September 15, 1944-Section II, page 13, Local news)

I wasn't aware of the situation but items such as coffee, sugar, fats, lard, butter, shoes and gasoline were being rationed. You received ration stamps in a booklet for each member of the family. I still have mine put away in a safe place. Victory gardens were starting up in neighborhoods so that you could grow your own vegetables, leaving farm-grown to be shipped to the soldiers and sailors overseas. The Sunday drive was eliminated due to the gas shortage. You were supposed to travel only if necessary.

There are over 5,000,000 women, "Rosie the Riveters" involved in the war effort.

My grandfather died in 1942 during the war. The knife business was left to my mom and grandmother to run. We were making knives for the war effort both for the mess-hall kitchens and GI mess kits. She now assumed a role of employer and business manager along with those of being a wife and mother of two children. In addition to this she was a driver for the Red Cross Motor

Pool with the responsibility of transporting pilots and their crews from the downtown hotels to the airbase at Hancock.

Edie, my mother-in-law, is also involved in the war effort on the assembly line at General Electric and working in the X-ray department at a local hospital. She will go on to run her own business as well, in **Tupperware**, starting from the ground floor as a dealer to winning the prestigious *Ad Astra* award as the top distributor in the entire nation. As with my mom, she too is married and will have children at home.

She stresses to me that they didn't have the luxuries in the kitchen that the homemaker of today has. Freezers, dishwashers, automatic washers and dryers, and small electric appliances had not yet been invented. **Betty Crocker** introduced a cake mix like mom used to make—add two eggs and beat! She maintains that was the beginning of women working without guilt. Those working in the factories now have money of their own and most importantly—independence!

The men are off to war in England where the beer is warm—*so are the women!*

The first woman who went to work on the floor of the New York Stock Exchange—was a good-looking, 18 year old redhead.

Women in service: Navy WAVES-82,000; Army WACS-92,500; Coast Guard SPARS-9,745; and CAA WASPS-487.

Popular slogan of that time:

> *"IF YOU BUY MORE BONDS, YOU GET MORE BOMBS"*

Bob Hope, the Andrew Sisters (Maxine, Patty, Laverne), Ginger Rogers, Jerry Colona, Rita Hayworth, Jimmy Durante, Jane Russell, Kate Smith, Dinah Shore, Will Rogers, Virginia Mayo, Rosemary Clooney, Bing Crosby, Patty Page, Jack Benny, Phil Harris, Betty Grabel, Marlene Dietrich, Barbara Hale, Gloria DeHaven, Carole Lombard, Alice Faye, Martha Raye, Heddy Lamar, Joey Brown, Edgar Bergen, Red Skelton, Danny Kaye, Ann Southern, Linda Darnell, Mickey Rooney, Duke Ellington, Olivia DeHaviland, Ann Sheridan, Kathryn Grayson, Anne Jeffreys, Ann Miller, James Cagney, Gary Cooper, Fred Astaire, Humphrey Bogart, Paulette Goddard, Al Jolson, June Allyson, Milton Berle, Deborah Kerr, Greer Garson, and Frances Langford all lend a hand in entertaining the troops on USO shows and raising money by selling war bonds.

The USO (United Service Organizations) was formed by the Salvation Army, YMCA, National Jewish Welfare Board, National Catholic Community Service, and the Travel Aid Association. It was independent from the government and sometimes went by the name Camp Shows, Inc.

Carole Lombard and Glenn Miller were both killed in plane crashes during the war.

Victory Gardens brought many a laugh from seed growers—one person bought a pound of turnip seed (enough to grow an acre), and there were requests for coffee seed and succotash seed. There are 18,000,000 backyard gardens in existence.

The "Dear John" letter comes to mean a letter of rejection from a former sweetheart, while a telegraph back to the family usually meant the death of a loved one serving overseas usually in these words:

"The Secretary of the War desires me to express his deep regret that your husband has been missing in action since…. If further details or other information are received, you will be promptly notified."

—The Adjutant General

31

LOCAL BOYS

It's nicer to receive a personal letter from a buddy that served with the spouse or boyfriend, as the following received by my wife's aunt, Anastasia.

"Soldier Tells Widow How Husband Died"

The following are excerpts from a letter Michael Klinowski wrote to Anastasia M. Zdep on June 26, 1945 to inform her of how her husband, William, died during World War II:

"We have just taken a hill in the Remagen bridgehead on the morning of March 13 and had begun as usual to dig in when we were immediately counterattacked by five enemy armored half-tracks. They were too close to our men to call for artillery so it was up to the bazooka to try and knock them out.

Bill and I were the only bazooka team left in the company so the task was left to us. Bill carried the rockets and he'd load and I'd fire. We only had four rockets left so we had to conceal ourselves by the road and allow them to come as close as possible to make sure each round counted.

I fixed at them when they got to about 20 yards or less. Bill kept loading and we made four direct hits, knocking out the first three and scoring a hit on the fourth, but it didn't put it out. At this point, the fourth and fifth halftracks turned around and headed back to their own lines, only to come back with German infantry in support later on with another counterattack.

But before they did, we done a little digging but not long enough so as we could get cover. Also we covered some very rough country and hills getting there that morning, so we didn't have very much strength left to do fast digging in, we were so exhausted.

Bill's hole was 10 feet behind mine and mine was about 15 feet away from the road when this second counterattack came, we had no way of or means of combating it as we had no more rockets left, so all the men withdrew behind the hill and jerries opened up with machineguns.

That is when, I believe, Bill got killed as he was trying to get cover with the rest of the boys.

It was already too late for me to try and make it with them so I laid in my hole which was only a little over a foot deep. Only one halftrack returned as the other one must have been partly disabled. This one stood directly in front of my hole on the road and with his three heavy machineguns sprayed lead in front and in back of my hole cutting the trees at their base all around me.

It was only a miracle that saved me. The halftrack crew must have thought perhaps that I was dead as I stayed still and prayed.

He stopped firing so I raised my head and looked out and saw him in front of me all buttoned up and when I looked to my left there were three (German soldiers) but not looking my way. They were only 20 feet from me and looking in the direction all the rest of the boys were, so they didn't notice me or else thought I was done for.

I still had one hand grenade left in my pocket so I quickly took it out, pulled the pin and threw it into the three of them and fled to where the boys were. One fired at me but missed. When I got back I looked for Bill but he couldn't be accounted for, so we thought then that he had been taken prisoner.

Meanwhile the jerries withdrew and we went back but couldn't find Zip. That was what we called him. I got one of the jerries with the grenade and also found the weapons laying there of the three krauts, so they must have been hit too.

Later we found him in the woods with machinegun bullets through his heart, so we're sure he met his death instantly. Enemy mortars and artillery were coming in on us very thick so we had to leave him where he was.

The next morning after being supplied again with ammo we moved out to attack, so just before I and another man carried him and placed him near the road and covered him with a raincoat, where he could be easily found. He showed no sign of suffering as I had my last look at him and offered a prayer then just before we had to move out. I still remember him in every one of my prayers and hope he rests in peace."

—(*The Post Standard* Friday, June 26, 1998)

William Zdep was my wife's uncle. He was posthumously awarded the Silver Star and a Bronze Star with a "V" for valor pin.

Six sons were born to Mary and Stanislaw Zdep. Three other brothers served during the war; Julian was shot down by the Japanese and parachuted into the safe hands of the Chinese; Walter served in the U.S. Army and was discharged for shell-shock from the service; Frank Zdep, my father-in-law, served in the U.S. Navy; Henry was too young to serve and Eddie was partially crippled from polio.

Frank's grand-daughters, Mackenzie and Chelsea Edgerton, donated a flag to the American Legion Post 141 of Manlius, in recognition of their grand-father, on Memorial Day, 2002. The flag had flown over the USS Arizona in Pearl Harbor, Hawaii and was purchased from the National Park Service in honor of those who lost their lives on that fateful day—December 7, 1941.

Gold stars are placed in front windows indicating the death of a son or daughter overseas.

People are slowly getting used to wearing polyester clothing.

Spam, powdered eggs, and baked beans are regulars on the mess hall menu.

American Television: (Not much to report as television is in its infancy.)

The American Broadcasting Company (ABC) is formed.

Births—Richard Moll, Kevin Dobson, Gary Burghoff, Bruce Weitz, Sharon Gless, Joan Van Ark, Chevy Chase, and Veronica Hamel.

American Literature:

Upton Sinclair was awarded the Pulitzer Prize for the novel, *"Dragon's Teeth"*.

Thornton Wilder was awarded the Pulitzer Prize for Drama, *"The Skin of Our Teeth"*.

Robert Frost was awarded the Pulitzer Prize for Poetry, *"A Witness Tree"*.

Beatrix Potter, the children's author, died.

Betty Smith writes, *"A Tree Grows in Brooklyn."*

American Sports:

Due to the war, there wasn't a great deal to report but I did find the following:

Navy beat Army in football (13-0) for the 2nd year in a row.

Yankees beat the Cardinals (4-1) in the World Series.

All American Girls Pro Baseball League, "A League of Their Own" starts.

Joe Namath and Arthur Ashe are born.

J. Longden aboard Count Fleet wins the Triple Crown in horse racing (5th horse to do so).

Jake LaMotta, in an upset, beats Sugar Ray Robinson in boxing.

Joe DiMaggio (NY Yankees) joins the Army as a volunteer inductee and goes on a coast-to-coast goodwill tour with Joe Louis.

300 colleges have dropped football during the war years.

Pete Gray returned home early from the war. He played baseball for the St. Louis Browns. He played in 77 games, batted .218, and had 51 hits—he lost an arm in the service!

In hockey, Detroit beats Boston 2-0, to win the Stanley Cup.

American Science:

On 2/4/43 there is a solar eclipse.

2/20/43 Paracutin Volcano erupts and buries the entire town of Parangaricutiro, Mexico.

The ENIAC computer is developed between the U.S. Army and the University of Pennsylvania.

The Colossus computer is developed by the British to break German codes.

George Washington Carver and Nikola Tesla both died.

Scientists led by J. Robert Oppenheimer are working on splitting the atom at Los Alamos, NM (The Manhattan Project). The project was proposed by Winston Churchill, funded by the U.S. under direction of FDR, and commanded by Brig. Gen. Leslie R. Groves.

Penicillin is successfully used in the treatment of chronic diseases.

Waksman and Schatz discover streptomycin.

American Aviation:

1/9 maiden flight of the Lockheed Constellation

1/27 The USAAF makes its first daylight raid on Germany.

7/13 maiden flight of the Curtis-Wright XP-55 Ascender

7/18 U.S. Navy airship K-74 is shot down by a German submarine.

8/1 USAAF B-24 bombers attack the oil refineries in Romania.

8/13 The USAAF makes its first bombing raid on Austria.

8/17 USAAF loses 59 planes over Regensburg and Schweinfurt.

32

"HERE'S LOOKING AT YOU KID"

American Film:

    Top grossing films of the year are: *For Whom the Bell Tolls, The Song of Bernadette* (Best Actress-Jennifer Jones), *This is the Army, Stage Door Canteen, Random Harvest, Star Spangled Rhythm, Casablanca* (Best Picture)

    Other films released: *Lassie Come Home, Heaven Can Wait, Madame Curie, Ivan the Terrible-Part I, Chicken Little.*

American Music:

    1/1/43 Frank Sinatra appears at the Paramount causing a mob scene of hysterical bobby-soxers to flood Times Square and blocking midtown New York City traffic for hours. Sinatra becomes a featured singer on the popular *"Your Hit Parade"* radio program.

    Jo Stafford and the Pied Pipers break away from the Tommy Dorsey Band and sign with the newly formed Capital Records. Perry Como signs with RCA. Miles Davis' musical career begins. The Carter Family disbands. Leonard Bernstein makes his debut conducting the NY Philharmonic Orchestra. Jazz musician "Fats" Waller died. Classical composer, Sergei Rachmaninov died.

Top Hits: *"As Time Goes By"*, *"I've Heard That Song Before"*, *"In the Blue of the Evening"*, *"Paper Doll"*, *"Pistol Packing Mama"*, *"Sunday, Monday, or Always"*, *"Taking a Chance on Love"*, *"There Are Such Things"*, *"When the Lights Go out Again"*, *"You'll Never Know"*.

Published Popular Music: *"All 'Er Nothin"*, *"Do Nothing Till You Hear From Me"*, *"Foolish Heart"*, *"I Cain't Say No"*, *"I'll Be Home For Christmas"*, *"It Could Happen To You"*, *"Kansas City"*, *"A Lovely Way To Spend An Evening"*, *"Mairzy Doats"*, *"Many A New Day"*, *"Oh, What A Beautiful Mornin"*, *"Oklahoma!"*, *"One For My Baby"*, *"Out Of My Dreams"*, *"People Will Say We're In Love"*, *"Poor Jud"*, *"Straighten Up And Fly Right"*, *"The Surrey With The Fringe On Top"*, *"You'll Never Know"*.

33

"ROCK AND ROLL IS HERE TO STAY"

You won't believe the following list of singers and musicians all born in the same year—1943:

Jim Croce, Janis Joplin, Dennis Edwards, Charles Winfield (Blood, Sweat & tears), Lou Christie, George Harrison (Beatles), George Benson, Mick Abrahams (Jethro Tull) Bobby Vee, Toni Tennille, Mary Wells (Supremes), Leslie Uggams, Bobby Harrison (Procol Harum), Little Eva, Florence Ballard (Supremes), Christine McVie (Fleetwood Mac), Bobby Sherman, Mick Jagger (Rolling Stones), Jerry Garcia (The Grateful Dead), Denis Payton (Dave Clark Five), David Soul, Dick Halligan (Blood, Sweat & Tears), Rosalind Ashford (Martha & The Vandellas), Joe Simon, Maria Muldaur, Joe Butler (Lovin' Spoonful), Steve Boone (Lovin' Spoonful), Julio Iglesias, Gary Alexander (The Association), Randy Bachman (Bachman-Turner Overdrive), Nick St. Nicholas (Steppenwolf), Jerry Martini (Sly & The Family Stone), Steve Miller (Steve Miller Band), Fred Turner (Bachman-Turner Overdrive), Ron Elliot (Beau Brummels), Joni Mitchell, Mike Smith (Dave Clark Five), Jim Morrison (The Doors), Chad Stuart (Chad & Jeremy), Dickey Betts (Allman Brothers Band), Grover Washington, Jr., Keith Richards (Rolling Stones), and John Denver.

How's that for talent! There are more, so if I've left off one of your favorites, I apologize. These are the ones that I recognize.

34

"THE GREAT WHITE WAY"

In the past few months PBS has been showing, *"Broadway—The American Musical"* on television in a six part series from 1920 to the present. We've survived the Great Depression where the musicals and dramas were about trying to make a living (survival) and escape with songs like, *"Brother Can You Spare a Dime?"* Yip Harburg said: "A song is the pulse of a nation. It's the fever chart of its health. Are we at peace, are we in trouble, is everything beautiful, or is it violent? Listen to our songs."

"Suppertime"—lynching in the South

"Stormy Weather"

"Let's Do It" and *"Anything Goes"*—all about hope (Cole Porter)

"I've Got Plenty of Nothing" from *Porgy and Bess* about the rural South by George Gershwin (music) and Ira Gershwin (lyrics)—according to FDR, 1/3 of the nation is ill housed and ill fed.

"Where or When"—lament senses a desperate population.

Irving Berlin's musical *"This Is the Army"* continues its popularity at the Broadway Theatre. Actual soldiers during the day were actors in the evening.

On Broadway and Off Broadway there are 97 productions running: 59 plays, 19 revivals, and 19 musicals.

Some theatres hold as few as 100 people, while others are much larger at the time entertaining 1,400 or more per matinee or evening performance. If you average it out at 750 patrons/performance times 97 productions, there are over 72,000+ people going to Broadway plays on any given night not counting matinee attendance! That is a lot of tickets no matter how you figure it.

Openings in 1943 include: *"Oklahoma"* (2,411), *"Kiss And Tell"*, *"The Two Mrs. Carrolls"*, *"The Merry Widow"*, *"One Touch Of Venus"* (567), *"The Skin Of Our Teeth"*, *"Carmen Jones"* (502), *"The Voice Of The Turtle"*, *"Outrageous Fortune"*, *"Early To Bed"* (380), *"The Lisbon Story"* (492), *"Show Boat"* (264), *"Sweet And Low"* (264) Performances are in parentheses. (en.wikipedia.org/wiki/1943)

"Oklahoma" by Richard Rogers and Oscar Hammerstein is the first time that music, story, dance, and setting are all integrated to tell a semi-serious story. This new approach triumphs, while the old style pretty much disappears. It runs for 2,411 performances and is #8 for longest running.

"The Voice Of The Turtle" by John Van Druten—are sophisticated stories of sex and love.

"The Skin of Our Teeth" by Thornton Wilder is a testimonial to man's ability to survive all disasters.

"Outrageous Fortune" by Rose Franken opened on 48th Street. It's about a wealthy Jewish family and their assorted problems. They have anxieties regarding homosexuality, discrimination, and the fear of death. (How ironic—little do they know!)

"Broadway-The American Musical" by PBS lists the following members of the MUSIC THEATRE HONOR ROLL: Harold Arlen, Irving Berlin, George Gershwin, Jay Gorney, Marc Blitzstein, Ira Gershwin, E.V. Harburg, Lorenz Hart, Dubose Heyward, Ted Koehler, Cole Porter, and Richard Rogers.

> "The pressures and tensions of the war created a need for escape among hard-working people on the home front—and one of the best places to get away from it all was New York City. There was more opportunity for enjoyment per square inch along the streets of mid-town Manhattan than anywhere else in the country, and servicemen in particular took full advantage of it. They swarmed over Times Square and Broadway, New York's 'Great White Way,' in search of live entertainment and the company of pretty girls. New York, in turn, came alive in a way never seen before.
> About 200 restaurants, serving some five million meals a week, catered to Time Square's bustling tourist trade. An evening was hardly complete

without a slice of Lindy's famous cheese cake or a cheese blintz at one of Broadway's many delicatessens. Over 50 nightclubs such as El Morocco and the Stork Club provided drinks and dancing to the music of the big bands, and audiences thrilled to the voice of a young crooner by the name of Frank Sinatra, who was appearing at the Paramount Theatre.... In 1943 alone more than 11 million people attended Broadway shows.... 'It was a public so anxious to attend the theatre that for a time it would attend anything playing in a theatre.'...for the excitement alone of an evening on Broadway was more than enough to make a serviceman's excursion to New York City worthwhile." (Bailey pg.16)

I remember my very first Broadway show, *"Peter Pan"* with Mary Martin and Cyril Richard at the Winter Garden Theatre. It was the start of many to come over the years.

"The Second World War, like the first, interrupted the theatre's normal patterns. Energies were turned to building morale and providing diversion. The war also raised serious doubts about a world which had created such horrors as the Nazi extermination camps and such destructive weapons as the atomic bomb. Out of the questioning would come new experiments in theatre and drama." (Brockett pg.641)

The plays went on during the war but the lights on Broadway had to be turned off for fear of German bombers.

"Broadway—The American Musical", on PBS, a fund-raising performance, prompts me to now look at what was else was going on in the world while we're having so much fun over here. Everything is not "swell" as they say in the plays and movies. This is the part of this book, where I guess you could say it changes to an "R" rating.

I once read that, "The only real crystal ball is your rear-view mirror." There is no way that anyone could have predicted what was to come that would literally affect millions of lives, other than those that perpetrated it. The plan is there in a writing titled, *Mein Kampf,* but nobody pays attention.

In 1859, Charles Dickens wrote, *"Tale of Two Cities"* and in that he said, "IT WAS THE BEST OF TIMES, IT WAS THE WORST OF TIMES", which I feel suits this time frame better.

III
DEMONS UNLEASHED

35

A NEW BOARD GAME

Just suppose that in early November of 1938, Germany came out with a new board game called, "SCAPEGOAT." The game would have been developed by its founders, that being: Hitler, Himmler, Heydrich, Hess & Company.

They have returned home from the Great War with bloody noses. They buy up all the bolts of brown cotton fabric that they can get their hands on. The first players are the "brown shirts."

Next, they need a sign of their purpose. I've got it—how about a cross with the ends bent and call it a "swastika!" That will be the emblem in the middle of the board for all the little characters to "boot-step" around.

Now they need a purpose for the game and someone to blame for losing the war and for the inflation they're experiencing and any other demented reasons they can concoct in the name of "Nationalism."

Ah Ha! What about the Jews? After all, they're only defenseless shop-keepers and merchants and don't own weapons. Besides that, they don't have the Nordic look. How could they be nice people if they lack the basic blonde hair and blue eyes? (Did you ever see a picture of Hitler with blonde hair?) These Judes are successful and have money; so a boycott of their stores should take care of that! Money means power.

Apparently the temples and synagogues are a threat to the community. November 9, 1938 is the night that is chosen to take away their places of worship. That particular evening, mass burnings and lootings are orchestrated across the country. From the intense heat, windows are blown out and the glass is broken (night of broken glass-hence, Kristallknacht).

"KRISTALLKNACHT" would be appropriate for the new version of hatred.

The SA, "brown shirts" now has partners to share in their dirty work. Himmler and Heydrich decide, with their boss's approval, of course, to form an elite group of black shirt, SS troops. So, if you haven't learned the rules of the game yet, the browns and blacks must be the "good guys" because everyone else needs to be—eliminated!

Let's identify the game pieces. "Oh" you say, "not just the Jews are to be dealt with?" Heck no, there are other harmless people out there that we might as well lump together. Anyone with common sense can tell you that Catholics, Romani gypsies, Jehovah Witnesses, homosexuals, Africans, political prisoners, and the handicapped and retarded have no right to live either. But if there are so many bad people out there, a plan is needed to deal with the problem.

Maybe a final solution is needed? That's it—A Final Solution! Why bother fooling around with stalling tactics—go for the throat! The final version of the game is to be titled, "HOLOCAUST" or "SHOAH" as the Jews call it; the demons and murderers are unleashed and run rampant across the board, and unchecked!

Propaganda tells the citizens that it's good for Germany. Go along with the new rules and you'll all prosper!

Oh, by the way, we're adding some acreage—there's no need for a banker as there won't be any mortgages. Just take what you need! They need the farm land of Poland, the wheat fields of the Ukraine, the Atlantic seaports of France, Belgium, Norway, and the Netherlands. There is a work force of 90,000,000 Slavs they can conscript for labor but first they'll address the Jewish and Catholic issue.

Elderly men and women aren't necessary. Same applies to children and the infirmed. Take the Jews and Catholics that are hated anyway, work them until they're exhausted and just dispose of them. Sounds simple but there are way to many to shoot and too many ditches to dig for mass graves.

The next plan is to round up these undesirables into a group and call for a "gasvagen." This is the new board piece. These are miniature gas chambers on wheels that respond to an area that has "problem people." They decorate the outside of the "gasvagens" with red crosses to simulate a relief organization that will remove them to a safer area. They're driven out in the woods. Then a hose is inserted into a hole in the side of the truck which is attached to the exhaust pipe. The verb is correct—they are "removed."

This procedure takes too much time and bodies must be buried to cover-up the crime. There are lots of words used at the time to explain away what is happening—elimination, extermination, liquidation, execution, purges, removal, but it is so simple to call it what it is—MURDER!

36

EUROPE BECOMES A GRAVEYARD

Months of research have gone into exploring this Holocaust issue and these are the figures that I have come up with. No person can ever say with certainty that these figures are accurate—incomplete records were kept of the murders. We can only come up with educated, conservative estimates.

> "Poland was chosen as the location for these camps for several reasons: firstly, it had by far the largest concentration of Jews in Nazi-occupied territories; secondly, it was located at a sufficient distance from prying German and other western eyes, yet was close enough to make feasible the transport of millions of Jews from other parts of Europe; thirdly, the Nazis had such deep contempt for the Poles that it was not considered unacceptable for Polish soil to be drenched in human blood-indeed the Polish nation, too, lost 6 million people during the Second World War, including the 3 million Polish Jews; and, lastly, the Nazis believed—as events turned out, with more than a little justification-that the level of religious and racial anti-Semitism among the ordinary Polish population was sufficiently high to suggest that they would remain aloof and indifferent to the Holocaust that was to be perpetrated in their own back yard." (Landau pg.176)

Number of Jews Murdered in Europe: An Estimate *

Country	Jewish Population September 1939	Number of Jews murdered	% of Jews murdered
Poland	3,300,000	2,800,000	85
Russia	2,100,000	1,500,000	71
Romania	850,000	425,000	50
Hungary	404,000	200,000	49
Czechoslovakia	315,000	260,000	82
France	300,000	90,000	30
Germany	210,000	170,000	81
Lithuania	150,000	135,000	90
Holland	150,000	90,000	60
Latvia	95,000	85,000	89
Belgium	90,000	40,000	44
Greece	75,000	60,000	80
Yugoslavia	75,000	55,000	73
Austria	60,000	40,000	66
Italy	57,000	15,000	26
Bulgaria	50,000	7,000	14
Others	20,000	6,000	30
Total	8,301,000	5,978,000	72

* Source: Leon Poliakov and Josef Wulf (eds), *Das Dritte Reich und die Juden: Dokumente und Aufsatze* (Arani-Verlag, GmbH, Berlin, 1955), cited in Paul Mendes-Flohr and Jehuda Reinharz, *The Jew in the Modern World* (Oxford University Press, 1980). (Laundau pg.316)

13,000,000 MURDERED: 6,000,000 Jews—3,000,000 of Polish nationality

3,000,000 from other countries

7,000,000 non-Jews—3,000,000 Polish Catholics

500,000 Romani gypsies

15,000 homosexuals

2,000,000 Russian prisoners

1,485,000 were retarded,

handicapped, political prisoners, degenerates, civic and spiritual leaders. These figures don't reflect the millions killed in service by all nations—61 million!

(www.secondworldwar.co.uk/casualty.html)

God must have been on vacation to allow this to happen. Anyway, I'm glad that I didn't have to play this board game—doesn't look like fun to me.

37

OSWIECIM a.k.a. AUSCHWITZ

"Death, death, death. Death in the morning, death in the afternoon, death at night. We lived with death."

—(Pavel Stenkin—Russian POW in Auschwitz)

"There was no God in Auschwitz. There were such horrible conditions that God decided not to go there"

—(Libusa Breder, Jewish prisoner, Auschwitz)

1/22/05

"Good Evening,
I have translated portions of the Auschwitz Museum booklet for you. I hope the piece will bring you a little closer to the prisoners' life struggles and heroism.
There is so much to talk about. I wish I had more time to investigate the dreadful stories of human cruelty on the part of the SS soldiers and the inspiring stories of human love and perseverance on the part of many of the prisoners.
Many of those people sacrificed their lives for others, for example Father Maximilian Colbe. Father Colbe, now a saint, volunteered to undergo deadly experiments instead of another man, who had a wife and children waiting for

him. Miraculously, the poison that the German doctors were experimenting with and which worked immediately on other people, could not kill Father Colbe for several weeks. They had to use other methods to put him to death. The man, whom Father Colbe saved, survived the camp.

Well, I would have typed my translation and edited it for you, but I got sick with flu. I will not be in church, but my husband is going to bring it instead. Please pick it up from him. I hope I am not too late with the translation.

Warmly, Julita

Good Evening,

I would like to let you know, that I have made several calls to find best sources of reliable information about the history of Auschwitz/Oswiecim concentration camp. I talked to people from Oswiecim government office, the Museum, and the publishing company. As a result of those conversations, I would like to suggest that you visit another web page: www.auschwitz.org.pl which is the official web page of the Oswiecim Museum. You can select the English version and find a wide variety of publications including English translations of historical documents, memoirs, videos, and DVDs.

The manager of the publishing company recommended the 5-volume chronicles that are also available through the Museum of the Holocaust in Washington. It would probably be less expensive to order directly from Poland. I will be more than happy to arrange it for you.

If you would like to call the Oswiecim Museum yourself, this is the phone number: 0-11-48-33-844-8123. The publisher's number is: 0-11-48-33-844-8054. I am also expecting some historical information that my parents sent me recently. I can translate it for you if you decide you might find it useful.

Best Wishes, Julita Klopocka-Niemiec

Here is the exact translation from the: *Panstwowe Muzeum w Oswiecimiu Auschwitz Austz Birkenau Informator* by Kazimierz Smolen in 1993 translated to English by Julita Klopocka-Niemiec in 2005.

"Built in 1940, the concentration camp in Auschwitz was intended to terrorize and exterminate the Polish. As time went by, Hitler's Germans sent there people from all European countries-mainly the Jews, but also Russian prisoners of war, the Gypsies, the Czecks, the Yugoslavs, the French, the Austrians, the Germans, and other nationalities.

Auschwitz (the German equivalent of Oswiecim, the name assigned in 1939) was Hitler's largest concentration camp for the Polish and the prisoners of other nations, whom the fascists condemned to isolation, gradual extermination by hard work, hunger, scientific experiments, as well as sudden death in individual and group executions. The number of exterminated victims is estimated around 1.5 million men.

At the gate of the main entrance are the words, 'ARBEIT MACHT FREI' (German for 'work makes one free'). Notice the B in ARBEIT is upside down-the prisoners' way to show protest.

After having locked up the door of a gas chamber (an area of about 210 square meters fit 2,000 victims) the SS soldiers threw Cyclon B from the ceiling. The people died within 15 to 20 minutes.

Before being put into a gas chamber, the victims had their golden teeth and jewelry removed and hair cut off.*

Cyclon B was manufactured by a German company "Degesch", which received about 300,000 marks for selling the gas during the years of 1941–1944. From 1942 to 1943 the gas chambers in Auschwitz used about 20,000 kg of Cyclon B. It took 5 to 7 kg of Cyclon B to kill 1,500 people.

All the arriving prisoners were told by the SS forces that there was no escape from the camp but through the chimney of a crematorium.* The new prisoners had all of their belongings taken away, hair shaved, and bodies disinfected. They were assigned numbers and registered. Beginning from 1943, the prisoners had their ID numbers tattooed in addition to wearing them on the uniform.

Depending on the reason for the arrest, the prisoners were assigned color coded triangles i.e. a red triangle indicated a political prisoner, a black triangle indicated a Gypsie, or a prisoner considered by the Germans as 'asocial'. A green triangle indicated criminals and a pink triangle indicated a homosexual. A purple triangle indicated a researcher of the Bible (Jehovah's Witness). The Jews were marked with the second yellow triangle (inverted) in a shape of a star.

All of the prisoners were dressed in light-weight striped uniforms which offered very little protection from the cold. The prisoners had their underwear changed once every several weeks or even months with no ability to do the laundry.

In addition to the crematoria, work was an effective way to kill prisoners. They built the camp, new barracks, roads, and later on were involved in a variety of sectors of the German industry.

One of the miseries of the camp life was an assembly, a summoning of the prisoners to count them. On July 6th, 1940 the assembly lasted 19 hours.

Sometimes, the prison SS management would order a penal assembly, during which they made the prisoners squat, or kneel, or hold hands up for long hours.

The prisoner's diet: 1,300 to 1,700 calories/day. Breakfast: ½ L. of coffee or herbal liquid. Dinner: 1L. Of meatless soup often prepared with rotting vegetables. Supper: 300–350 gm. of stale dark, clumpy bread with 20 gm. of sausage or 30 gm. of margarine or cheese. (Apparently no Lindy's cheesecake for these unfortunates)

The prisoners suffered and often died of malnutrition. On the day of liberation, the women weighed 25–35 kg.

The children who arrived at the camp with their parents, mainly Jewish, Gypsies, Polish, and Russian were treated like adults. The majority of them perished in gas chambers. Very few selected children were obliged to follow the rigors of the camp routine. Some of them i.e. twins were used in deadly experiments, others had to work hard.

The living conditions in the camp were catastrophic. The first prisoners slept on concrete covered with straw. Later, straw mattresses were used. 200 prisoners slept in barracks that would hardly fit 40–50 people.

The space between barracks 10 and 11 is fenced with a tall wall on both sides. Wooden screens on the windows prevented other prisoners from witnessing executions. SS soldiers shot several thousand prisoners, mainly Polish, there. Before executions, the prisoners had to take off their clothes. Other forms of punishment included whipping and hanging by hands twisted in the back. Barrack 11 was isolated from the rest of the camp, since the camp prison was located in the basement.

Despite cruel living conditions, endless terror and danger, the prisoners conspired against the SS. Mainly, they maintained contact with local Polish people, who brought them food and medications. The prisoners shared information on the crimes committed in the prison, gave out names of the prisoners, the SS men, evidences of crimes, and exchanged encrypted correspondence.

The resistance movement's goal was to eliminate the prisoners who blindly cooperated with the Germans and replace them with war prisoners. The prisoners helped one another with food supplies. They organized cultural events, such as conspiratorial meetings, discussions, poetry recitals, art work, and celebrated masses.

Birkenau was a satellite camp located 3 km away from the main camp. 300 barracks were built there to accommodate 100,000 prisoners (in August 1944).

The plagues of the camp included: lack of water, catastrophic hygiene conditions, and throngs of rats.

*I question that gold teeth were removed prior to the gas chamber as the Germans were trying to portray an air of normalcy to keep the efficiency of the death machine functioning at peak. My research shows jaw smashing after death but I wasn't there to challenge what someone asserts. Also, I find nothing to indicate that prisoners were told in advance what was to happen to them. An orchestra would often play to keep the situation calm.

If you should do further research on your own, here according to the museum are the satellite camps for Oswiecim-Brzezinka (Auschwitz-Birkenau): Blachownia Sl.(Blechhammer), Bobrek, Bruntal (Freudenthal), Chorzow (Konigshutte), Czechowice-Dziedzice—2, Gliwice—4, Goleszow (Golleschau), Hajduki (Bismarckhutte), Harmeze, Jawiszowice, Jaworzno, Kobior (Kobier), Ledziny-Lawki, Libiaz Maly, Lagiewniki (Hubertushutte), Lagisza Cmentarna (Lagischa-Grube), Monowice, Myslowice (Furstengrube), Plawy (Plawy), Prudnik (Neusstadt), Rajsko, Rybnik (Charlottengrube), Siemianowice (Laurahutte), Sosnowiec, Stara Kuznia (Althammer), Swietochlowice (Eintrachtshutte), Trzebinia, Zabrze (Hindenburg), Pszczna (Pless). I assume the Polish name is first, followed by the name given by the Germans.

There were over 1,000 concentration/extermination camps constructed throughout Germany and Poland but the most notorious was KL AUSCHWITZ. This camp was located in and around the town of Oswiecim, Poland which the Germans pronounced as Auschwitz and renamed it as such during the war. It consisted of three main camps and several smaller, associated camps.

The first constructed was KL Auschwitz I (STAMMLAGER) which became the living quarters and administration buildings for the feared SS (Schutzstaffel). It also housed and murdered non-Jewish prisoners at the outset (estimates of 3,000,000 Catholics). Several buildings were already in existence since these were stables for the Polish Army Cavalry.

Next to be built was the operational center called KL Auschwitz II-(BIRKENAU) just outside of Brzezinka. Here is where the train tracks ended. Trains pulling cattle cars full of humans arrived daily from all over Europe. ** BIRKENAU buildings became the site of the greatest MASS MURDER in the history of humanity—eight gas chambers, forty-six ovens, and approximately 4,400 corpses per day!

"Polish Christians and Catholics were actually the first victims of the notorious German death camp. For the first 21 months after it began in 1940, Auschwitz was inhabited almost exclusively by Polish non-Jews. The first ethnic Pole died in June 1940 and the first Jew died in October 1942.

—(www.holocaustforgotten.com)

KL Auschwitz III (MONOWITZ) or KL Auschwitz III (BUNA) as they were known, was the location of the experimental labs and chemical and pharmaceutical production under the direction of the conglomerate, I.G. Farben, located at Monowice, 2 miles to the east of which I'll talk about later—stay tuned!

38

DIDN'T KNOW OR DIDN'T CARE

Because of the obliteration of the Polish press by the Nazis, most of the world was not aware, including many parts of Nazi-occupied Poland, of the atrocities going on. Even to this day, much documentation of the Holocaust is not available. The entire records of Auschwitz were stolen by the Soviets and not returned. It was Hitler's goal to rewrite history.

"You could have read the front page of The New York Times in 1939 and 1940, she (Laurel Leff) wrote, 'without knowing that millions of Jews were being sent to Poland, imprisoned in ghettos, and dying of disease and starvation by the tens of thousands. You could have read the front page in 1941 without knowing that the Nazis were machine-gunning hundreds of thousands of Jews in Russia.'

'You could have read the front page in 1942 and not have known that the Germans were carrying out a plan to annihilate European Jewry. In 1943, you would have been told once that Jews from France, Belgium, and the Netherlands were being sent to slaughterhouses in Poland and that more than half of the Jews of Europe were dead, but only in the context of a single story on a rally by Jewish groups that devoted more space to who had spoken than to who had died.'

'In 1944, you would have learned from the front page of the existence of horrible places such as Maidanck and Auschwitz, but only inside the paper could you find that the victims were Jews. In 1945, [liberated] Dachau and Buchenwald were on the front page, but the Jews were buried inside.'

A story buried but not, over time, forgotten."

—(Racematters.org 2/21/05)

Marvin Kalb wrote *"The Journalism of the Holocaust"* and I extract and quote a very small portion.

"On May 18, 1942, The New York Times reported from Lisbon that the Germans had machine-gunned more than 100,000 Jews in the Baltic states, another 100,000 in Poland, twice that many in western Russia. The news appeared on an inside page—several inches of neutral copy.

In May, two Jewish members of the Polish National Council in Poland—Szmul Zygielbojm and Ignacy Schwarzbart—produced even more startling information. They disclosed that the Germans, with Teutonic efficiency, had begun to put Jews into what were called concentration camps there, to be killed in gas chambers, 90 at a time, or burned to death in ovens. Zygielbojm and Schwarzbart concluded that the Nazis had embarked on a program, as they put it, 'To annihilate all the Jews in Europe.' The two Jewish representatives recommended that the Allies retaliate in some way against German citizens living within their jurisdictions. The recommendation fell on deaf ears, coming as it did, after all, from 'prejudiced sources.'

News of the Nazi atrocities was published on June 30, 1942 and again on July 2. The New York Times ran reports, first published by the Daily Telegraph in London, that more than 1,000,000 Jews had already been killed by the Germans. The reports were mind blowing, but The Times again placed them on an inside page."

—(ushmm.org/lectures/kalb.htm2/21/05)

39

TWO JEWS

Jesus, a Jew, appeared on this earth, in human form, some 2,000+ years ago as the Son of GOD.

Adolf Schicklgruber, a Jew, was born April 20, 1889 as one of 6 children born to Klara Polzl and Alois Schicklgruber. The father, Alois, was an illegitimate son of Maria Anna Schicklgruber of Strones, a rural area of Austria. There is speculation that the grandfather, a wealthy Jew, who had a relationship with Maria Anna, had a last name of either Frankenberger or Frankenreither. Illegitimacy in lower Austria was common at the time and in rural areas ran as high as forty per cent. Children were the lifeblood of any farm and every healthy worker was welcome.

Alois legitimized his name in 1876 as Hitler and took as his third wife, his niece—Klara. They produced 6 children, Gustav, Ida, Otto, Adolf, Edmund, and Paula. Hitler forbade geneticists from going too deeply into his background. The story got started that Hitler was trying to hide something. It was not only the potential Jewish situation but it was the fact there was a history of mental illness in his ancestry as well as certain relationships and marriages that bordered on incest.

"One of Hitler's henchmen, Hans Frank, declared during the Nuremberg Trials in 1945 that Hitler's grand-mother had worked in the town of Graz as a servant in the home of a Jewish family named Frankenberger. He further claimed that she was seduced by the head of the household and that Hitler's father was the result of that liaison."

—(Mazal veritas3.holocaust-history.org)

"It seems that Jews don't want to believe that Hitler could have been Jewish himself. For him to commit such acts on his own kind is hard to fathom.

In a special report dated 1/19/05 by Guardian Unlimited written by Susanna Loof of Associated Press, she writes: "One of the thousands of victims of the Nazi regime's program to kill mentally ill people was a relative of Adolf Hitler, two historians said yesterday.

The woman, identified only as Alosia V., was 49 when she was gassed to death on December 6, 1940 in Hartheim Castle near the northern Austrian city of Linz, Timothy Ryback said.

Mr. Ryback, an American who now lives in Salzburg and heads the Obersalzberg Institute in Berchtesgaden, Germany, said the details surrounding the woman's death surfaced last week, after Obersalzberg archivist Florian Beieri gained access to her medical file at a Vienna medical institution where she had been treated.

An ink stamp on the file serves as 'proof of extermination,' Mr. Ryback said. 'It's painful to see what this woman went through. It highlights the cruelty and brutality of that system to an excruciating degree.'

That mental illness flourished in Hitler's extended family is nothing new. A 1944 Gestapo report, known for decades, described Aloisia's line of the family as 'idiotic progeny,' Mr. Beieri said.

Recently released medical files on her, say she had schizophrenia, depression, delusions and other mental problems, Mr. Ryback said. Her treatment included confinement in cage beds, a practice that was widespread even before Nazi times. It is unclear whether Hitler was aware of his relative's illness and fate, Mr. Ryback added.

Aloisia was the great-grandchild of the sister of Hitler's paternal grandmother, meaning she was part of the Schicklgruber side of the family, Mr. Beieri said. Her family was close to Hitler's, and the Nazi leader's father helped her father get a job as a civil servant in Vienna, he added.

In five years of research the two historians kept coming across 'cases of either physical or mental disabilities in Hitler's family.' The Schicklgrubers were especially hard hit and 'crashed into suicide and mental illness."

To show part of the perversion in the man, he showed interest mostly in young girls, not too bright, that could not question his actions or politics. His first attraction that we know about was Maria Reiter who attempted to commit suicide at age 16. Next was Geli Raubal, his 19 year old niece, who shot herself in the heart at age 20 after finding a letter to Hitler from Eva Braun. Next of the mentally unbalanced girl friends was Renate Mueller who was an actress in Berlin. She too committed suicide by leaping out of a hotel window. Eva was the one who, for whatever reason, stuck with him until the end. She too had attempted suicide in 1932 by shooting herself in the neck. She ultimately took her own life in the bunker in Berlin at the end of the war.

By 1942, Hitler had become a regular methamphetamine user, receiving daily injections of Pervitid. This was in addition to narcotic pills for sleeping. At one point he was taking 28 different medications—quite a cocktail of drugs causing increasing erratic behavior. In addition to this was the suspicion of syphilis from years of womanizing.

According to a 1943 report from the Office of Strategic Services, his relations with his own niece, Geli, were most bizarre. This book may be read by young people so I'm not going to describe his perversions here. Suggested readings are at the conclusion for your own edification. (www.rotten.com/library/bio/nazi/adolf-hitler/)

The way he viewed himself is pretty much summed up in part of a speech that he gave at Nuremburg, "The fact that you found me among millions is a miracle, the fact that I found you, is your good fortune." He was good at making speeches but not at running the government. His office and cabinet room were never used at the Reichschancelory.

The true power was handed over to his main henchmen those being "Borman, von Ribentrop, Mueller, Frank, Funk, Jodl, Keitl, Ley, Streicher, Rosenberg, Schacht, Frick, Fritsche, von Neurath, and the more notorious Himmler, Heydrich, Goebbles, Hess, Speer, Eichmann, and Mengele." (Simon Wiesenthal Center/Museum of Tolerance)

His corps of officers ruled like the way they thought he'd want them to rule. All were striving for his favor. Probably due to all the medication he was taking, he wouldn't have been able to use sound judgment, even if he wasn't insane. Another expression was, "What can be committed verbally should never be put in writing."

Should you ever do research on your own; there are many derivations on Hitler such as, Hidlar, Hidlarcek, Hydler, Hytler, Hidler, and Hiedler.

Adolf grew up in a small town called Lambach where they lived across the street from a Benedictine monastery. The monastery's coat of arms featured a bent cross, a swastika!

> Hitler wrote, "How must the man be constituted who will lead Germany back to her old heights? The man should be a dictator not averse to the use of slogans, street parades and demagoguery. He must be a man of the peo-

ple yet have nothing in common with the mass. Like every great man, he must be 'all personality,' and one who 'does not shrink from bloodshed. Great questions are always decided by blood and iron.' To reach his goal, he must be prepared 'to trample on his closest friends', dispense law 'with terrible hardness' and deal with people and nations 'with cautious and sensitive fingers' or if need be trample on them with the boots of a grenadier." (Toland pg.124.)

The shame of Germany's surrender on November 11, 1918 in the forest of Compiegne overwhelmed him. Life seemed unbearable...he heard voices summoning him to save Germany—that's what he said, anyway.

Anyhow, in my opinion, he appeared as the son of Satan—can you think of anyone in the history of the world that was more evil or demonic? Certainly no other human disrupted so many lives in our time or stirred so much hatred.

To his faithful followers he was a hero, to the rest he is still a madman, an evil murderer.

—(Toland pgs.3–12)

I don't want to offend anyone by using a comparison of Jesus and Hitler. I'm merely showing opposite ends of the spectrum. One had extreme love for mankind. The other couldn't wait to murder all of us. He even forecast the fate of his own people by making young boys and old men go up against battle-hardened troops of England, Canada, America and Russia when the end was near.

I'm not going to write another biography on Hitler, I feel he's had way too much attention already but I do want to reinforce to this generation and those to come, what a monster was in our presence while I was a youth. He was not the figment of someone's imagination, but a real living, breathing person of our time. It would be interesting to speculate how history would have been written had Hitler been accepted to architectural studies rather than to have been judged a failure early in his life.

I have a daughter who is a sophomore in high school taking junior honors courses, one of them being World History, now called Global Studies. Her text book is over 1,000 pages but with only 21 pages on WW II and of that ½ page devoted to the Holocaust—2 paragraphs—that's it! History books give you the facts but not the emotions. I asked her if she knew if any of her friends watched educational television such as The History Channel, and her response was negative.

That's what we're up against.

40

WHEN FREE WILL IS SURPRESSED, THE SPIRIT IS TAKEN AWAY

It's pretty much all over for the Jews, Catholics, Jehovah's Witnesses, Romani gypsies, Russian prisoners, retarded, handicapped, homosexuals, Jesuits, priests, clergy, educated, and anyone who spoke up against the Nazi regime. The SA and SS have the power to do what they want—unchecked. The hounds have been released!

The Germans attack Poland from the West and the Russians do the same from the East. Poles are rounded up and placed into ghettos. The educated, such as the Jesuits, who question this new authority, are locked into concentration camps. The ghettos become a holding tank, so to speak, until decisions are made as to what is to become of all these prisoners. The Germans have had their eye on Poland for some time as the new territory for development of the "master race."

In the early stages of the Holocaust, the Polish Catholics were the dartboard. On August 22, 1939, a few days before the official start of World War II, Hitler authorizes his commanders, with these famous words, to kill "without pity or mercy, all men, women, and children of Polish descent or language. Only in this way can we obtain the living space (lebensraum) we need."

"Young Polish men were forcibly drafted into the German army. The Polish language was forbidden. Polish churches and synagogues were burned.

The priests were arrested and sent away to concentration camps. Polish towns and cities were renamed in German.

At the onset, thousands of Polish community leaders, mayors, local officials, teachers, lawyers, judges, senators, and doctors were executed in public. The first mass execution of World War II took place in Wawer, a town near Warsaw, Poland on December 27, 1939 when 107 Polish non-Jewish men were taken from their homes in the middle of the night and shot. This was the beginning of the street round-ups and mass executions that continued throughout the war.

—(www.holocaustforgotten.com/poland)

Poland was simultaneously attacked by both the Nazis and the Russians. The country was divided in two and each was as ruthless as the other in there treatment of captives. During this reign of terror, Poland lost 45% of the doctors, 57% of attorneys, 40% of professors, 30% of technicians, 18% of clergy, and most of the journalists.

—(Dr. Richard C. Lucas)

41

POLES, JEWS, and LAKOTA

Polish people were classified by the Nazis according to their racial characteristics. Those who appeared Aryan were deported to Lodz and the children were placed in Aryan homes to be raised as Germans. Many were sent to Germany to work in slave labor camps. The balance went to Auschwitz.

Polish Christians and Catholics were the first victims of the notorious death camps. The Holocaust is usually taught as the mass genocide of almost 6 million Jews but more than 7 million others were killed including over 3 million Catholics. They too deserve their place in history not to be forgotten. (www.holocaustforgotten.com)

Jehovah Witnesses refused to take an oath of loyalty to the Nazi ideology and were imprisoned as "dangerous traitors" and forced to wear purple arm bands. They, like the Catholics, were persecuted and murdered for not recognizing Hitler as a god-like figure. The Romani gypsies were looked upon, as the Jews, as inferior, nomadic, and worthless. Almost the entire Eastern European population of gypsies, ½ million, were murdered as well.

The "master race" had no room right from the start for any person with homosexual tendencies—even his own SS personnel suspected of being gay were imprisoned, humiliated, and then murdered. They were to wear pink triangles on their prison uniforms for identification. (www.holocaustforgotten.com/non-jewishvictims.htm)

After World War I, the French, during the occupation, brought people of African descent into Germany. Some of these Africans married white German women. Hitler called the children of these relationships, "Black Disgrace" in

his book," *Mein Kampf*." These children, mulattos, were taken to the Number 3 Commission which promptly sent them to hospitals for sterilization without the parent's permission. Hitler felt no moral duty to offspring of a foreign race.
(Carol Aisha Blackshire-Belay, Terese Pencak Schwartz, Ina R. Freidman, Dr. Richard C. Lucas Stefan Korbonski)

Hitler had paid particular attention to the way that Native Americans were treated in the United States. This unchecked genocide of indigenous people intrigued him.

Property could just be taken away without payment, treaties weren't honored, and tribes were located on pseudo concentration camps called "reservations." Natives died of starvation and disease.

> "Hitler was aware of the American assault on Native populations through his life-long reading and re-reading of the German, cowboy-western, novelist Karl May (he was still reading May in his bunker years later in the war). He connected May's 'Redskins' with the Russian natives explicitly in another of his table talks: Speaking of what he called 'this Russian desert', he asserted, 'We shall populate it…. We'll take away its character of an Asiatic steppe, we'll Europeanize it. With this object, we have undertaken the construction of roads that will lead to the southernmost point of the Crimea and to the Caucasus. These roads will be studded along their whole length with German towns, and around these towns our colonists will settle. 'As for the natives': We'll have to screen them carefully. The Jews, that destroyer, we shall drive out…
>
> And above all no remorse on this subject! We're not going to play children's nurses; we're absolutely without obligation as far as these people are concerned…
>
> There's only one duty: to Germanize this country by the immigration of Germans, and to look upon the natives as Redskins…
>
> In this business I shall go straight ahead, cold-bloodedly…I don't see why a German who eats a piece of bread should torment himself with the idea that the soil that produces this bread has been won by the sword. When we eat wheat from Canada, we don't think about the despoiled Indians.
>
> Such conquest had been rationalized long before by apologists for imperialism."
>
> —(Rhodes pg.93)

On December 12th of 1890, the U.S. Army under the command of General Miles, Colonel Forsyth, and Major Whiteside, set out to slaughter and eliminate men, women, and children of the Lakota Sioux tribe. The slaughter (notice: I'm not using the term, battle) took place just outside of the Pine Ridge Reservation at a place called Wounded Knee Creek. Men, women, and children, were cut down from behind as they fled the cavalry charge and canon fire.

Days later, civilians were paid $2.00 per body to throw frozen corpses into mass graves (sound familiar?).

The British philosopher, Herbert Spencer, in 1850 wrote, "taking no account of incidental suffering, exterminate such sections of mankind as stand in their way...Be he human or be he brute, the hindrance must be got rid of".

Darwin in 1864 compared the "lower" races to weeds—the extermination of populations, he contended, was a form of natural selection.

42

IT CONTINUES

In 1940, France is the next country to be invaded by the Germans. On June 16th of that year, Marshal Henri Philippe Petain succeeds Paul Reynaud as Premier of France and shortly thereafter asks the Germans for an armistice which was concluded on June 22.

On July 2nd, with the consent of the Germans, he established his government in Vichy in central France. On July 10th he assumed the title of Chief of State, ruling thereafter with dictatorial powers over that portion of France not directly under German control.

> He established a Fascist government that became notorious for its collaboration with German dictator, Adolf Hitler. It wasn't long before they passed anti-Semitic laws and rounded up French, Spanish, and Eastern European Jews who were deported to German concentration camps. Some of these people that were arrested had fled to France earlier to escape the Nazis and now were being handed over for slave labor and ultimate murder.
>
> Petain was arrested after the war and sentenced to death. His sentence was later commuted to life imprisonment which is where he died.
>
> —(Worldatwar.net/biography/p/petain)

Those rounded up were assigned:
Red triangles for political prisoners under supervision
Green triangles for common criminals
Black triangles for relapsed criminals or unwanted Africans
Pink triangles for homosexuals

Purple triangles for Jehovah Witnesses
Yellow triangles (inverted) for Jews

These Jewish men and women in France are told to bring valuables with them in a suitcase as they won't be safe left behind. They are to bring enough money with them to last for several weeks. The children, they are told, will be cared for and will join them later—not here, but in the hereafter. They don't know this and will never know.

As many people as a cattle car can accommodate, are crowded in standing up so that more can fit. A five gallon pail is to be used as a latrine for all these people over the next two day and two night journey to Auschwitz. There is no room to sit and no one wants to lie down in human excrement on the floor.

They hadn't been told ahead of time how long the trip would be, or to bring their own food and water with them. Some revert to drinking their own urine. There are quite often railroad delays making the journey longer than the Germans planned. In the summer months, the prisoners are very dehydrated and overheated from lack of ventilation. During the winter transportation, the prisoners freeze as there are no heaters on board and quite often the train sits at the railroad siding in sub-zero conditions for many hours.

Upon arrival at Auschwitz, the train pulls up to the RAMPA (ramp) where the doors are unlocked and the survivors of the trip are greeted with whips and biting dogs.

"The ramp was surrounded by flowering plants in good weather. An orchestra composed of internees—all young and pretty girls, dressed in white blouses and navy blue skirts—played during the "selection."

—(The Holocaust pg.689)

Here is where the famous SELEKTION (selection) takes place. Everyone is forced to line-up in a long row where "doctors" examine the prisoners as to their physical condition. Most generally, younger, fit men and some women without children are told to go in one direction whereas the elderly, the ill, the women with children are sent in another direction. For all eternity they will never see each other again until they meet in the kingdom of God, if that is your belief.

Doctor Mengele has his eyes on youngsters that are twins, for his own diabolical needs.

Seamstresses and tailors are kept alive to make SS uniforms from material collected later. The young, pretty girls are sorted out for the camp whorehouse or the SS barracks where they are repeatedly raped and molested. Others catch the eye of the deviant female guards and Russian trustees until it is their time to fuel the furnaces.

The "selected" men are lead to barrack-like buildings where they'll spend their time when not working. There are bunks arranged three high to accommodate 9 men in very cramped quarters. This figure will change as the Holocaust accelerates.

There is very little running water and virtually no place to clean up. Timepieces and calendars had been removed, so that the days of the week became one long period of hard labor. There were no designated days, no measures of time.

Their day starts very early in the morning with APPELL (roll call) outdoors which is pretty gruesome in the winter weather as prisoners are not allowed to have coats or sweaters. Clothes brought with them on the train were confiscated, fumigated with ZYKLON-B (hydrogen cyanide), and sent to Germany.

A small loaf of bread to feed 8 people plus a lukewarm cup of crushed acorn coffee constitutes breakfast. The pail that is used to serve the coffee, is the same one used at night for a portable latrine as prisoners are not allowed outside.

Work details are assigned for the day. Slave labor was used for cleaning toilets, collecting clothing for delousing, washing floors, building railroad tracks, hauling stones, piling wood, and digging graves.

The worst detail is SONDERKOMMANDO. These inmates are responsible for emptying out the gas chambers and loading the bodies in the ovens for burning. They quite often saw their own dead relatives. The KANADA detail would work all day sorting clothes, emptying suitcases, and looking for valuables which the SS would steal and take home.

—(History1900s.about.com/library/holocaust/blauschwitz.htm)

They might later be served a soup of lukewarm water and usually spoiled potatoes. Any fat tissue they had on their bodies when they arrived is used up first and then the metabolism breaks down muscle tissue. Whatever sleep they get is with fleas, ticks, rats, lice, and other parasites as bed companions.

At Auschwitz, the word is spread quickly that prisoners who go on sick leave at the hospital (gold-brickers), don't ever return. An eyewitness tells of these prisoners being held up while a doctor injects 5cc of phenol, evipan, sepso, or gasoline from a long needle directly into the heart causing immediate death. Others go to the hospital for experimental surgery where the stomachs that had not been sewn up properly, come in contact with soiled and lice-infested blankets. The mattresses they are to lie on are usually fouled with excrement from diarrhea-stricken patients. These bodies are removed at night and disposed of in the ovens. I guess the Hippocratic Oath doesn't mean anything.

43

TAKE A NUMBER

Those that did not go in the direction with the young men to work details are lead to other buildings. The women with long hair immediately get a close haircut. Here they are all told to select a hook on the wall for their belongings and to remember the number after they come out of the "showers." They need one after that train ride. It is a ploy to keep orderliness and this false hope keeps the death machine moving along.

Prisoners are to strip naked in front of each other. Men, women, children, elderly have been further humiliated right to the end! They are moved into a room that resembles a shower, complete with false plumbing. The doors are closed and locked behind them. They are to be killed, like fleas on their clothing—no prayers—no last words—no chance to say "good-bye." They are to be murdered just because some son-of-a-bitch maniac says that it is "good" for Germany.

Depending on the facility, the Zyklon-B is dropped from either the ceiling or through an opening in the wall. No matter, death fumes immediately pour out of the canisters and fill the lungs of helpless humans. Eyewitnesses say that the gas settles to the floor first, so that when the doors are opened a few minutes later, the bodies are in a pyramid shape as they tried to climb to the ceiling for fresh air.

Before being carried off to the crematorium, the mouths of the corpses are examined for hidden jewelry or gold teeth. The jaws are smashed with hammers to collect the gold. At least they waited until they died!

The Nizkor Project is one of the most thorough reports that I have read in my research. It is an 18 page paper by Brian Harmon on the *TECHNICAL ASPECTS OF THE HOLOCAUST: Cyanide, Zyklon-B, and Mass Murder.* The structure of the paper is such:

Part one: Physiological Basis of Cyanide Poisoning

    A. Cells and energy

    B. Cytochromes in the Electron Transport System

    C. How Cyanide Kills

    D. Data on Cyanide

Part two: Use of Zyklon-B

    A. Extrapolate from Nuremburg doc N1-9912

    B. A Hypothetical Gassing

    C. Compare to Existing Documents

Conclusion

The report is lengthy and extremely technical so I won't use the entire text but in his own words I quote verbatim:

> "Because many Holocaust deniers find themselves unable to dismiss the many volumes of historical information documenting the Holocaust, they often turn to other methods. A very common tactic is to claim that the Holocaust was 'technically impossible,' improperly citing chemical and physical data as 'proof'.... I hope to provide the knowledge necessary to take on Holocaust denier's claims directly, so they can easily be discredited by anyone.
>
> Hydrogen Cyanide acts by inhibiting tissue oxidation, that is, by preventing useful employment of oxygen carried by the blood. Cyanide binds cytochromes more tightly than oxygen, and as a result is lethal at very low concentrations, at about 300 ppm.
>
> The effect also occurs at hemoglobin, as cyanide will bind to that too, preventing oxygen from reaching cells. In essence, this is how cyanide kills cells and whole organisms. Cyanide is most effective on warm-blooded animals such as mammals, but is less effective on insects.
>
> Here's what the 10th edition (1983) of the Merck Index had to say on Hydrogen Cyanide: Hydrocyanic acid, Blauseare, prussic acid, colorless gas

or liquid, characteristic odor, very weakly acidic, burns in air with a blue flame. INTENSELY POISONOUS MIXED WITH AIR...death may result from a few minutes exposure to 300 ppm. 'MUST BE HANDLED BY SPECIALLY TRAINED EXPERTS.'

**For fumigation purposes, a German firm called Degesch made a product called Zyklon-B. Zyklon-B consisted of liquid HCN (Hydrogen Cyanide) adsorbed onto a carrier—'wood fiber disks, dia gravel, or small blue cubes. Although toxic, cyanide was hard to detect alone, so an irritant was added to the Zyklon to warn people of exposure.

A 'typical' can of Zyklon contained 200 grams of HCN adsorbed onto the carrier, and was stored in metal tins marked with a death's head and warning that read: 'Giftgas' (Deathly poisonous gas). Zyklon-B shipments to Nazi death camps had the warning indicator removed, which would prevent people from detecting the gas's presence before it was too late.... 'one mg per kg of body weight is sufficient to kill a human being.'

The fact that the irritant indicator was removed from shipments to Nazi death camps is another curious feature, as one would wonder why an obvious safety feature would be removed from a product if its intended use was purely benign.

Imagine a room with 210 square meters of floor space...I'll simply assume that the walls are 2.5 meters high, so the building will have a total volume of 525 cubic meters.

The structure would be fitted with vents on the ceiling for pouring in the Zyklon, and exhaust fans would be used to clear the room once gassing was completed. This structure would be largely below ground, to help maintain a constant temperature using the earth as insulation.... With only one gassing a day, plenty of time will be left for ventilating the gas chamber and moving the bodies to the crematoria for combustion.

The next question is, given one gassing a day and four gas chambers at the camp, how many people can be killed in a time period of one and one half years (18 months)? I choose this time period since the four large extermination facilities at Auschwitz-Birkenau were in operation from 1943 until their destruction by the fleeing Nazis in November 1944. For the sake of argument, I'll say that's about 1 ½ years (May 1943 to Nov. 1944).

If the gas chambers were in operation for 548 days (1 ½ years), the total dead would be: 840 x 4 x 548= 1,841,280 based on 840 people/room/killing."(Krema 2, 3, 4, 5)

If you add to Mr. Harmon's figures those that died from firing squads, starvation, torture, and disease, the figures for Auschwitz alone are staggering. He is not even factoring in Crematoria Bunkers 1 and 2, not calculated in the equation.

44

ENTER ON A TRAIN—EXIT UP THE CHIMNEY

In the first stages of the Holocaust, prisoners were led or driven out to the woods to be shot and burned in pits. This was the stage after the "gasvagens," which also took too much time. Himmler noticed that pests on inmates clothing subjected to Zyklon-B fumigation, died right away, which led him to believe of the same effects on humans. The ovens were necessary not only for disposal purposes but also to remove evidence. If you were of the wrong race, nationality, religion, or political affiliation by German standards, you disappeared in smoke! Jews accounted for 80% of all deaths at Auschwitz.

The bodies were thrown on to carts for transportation to the ovens. Here again, there is no respect for the dead. They are treated like cord wood—just a fuel. The hair that was cut will be sent back to Germany for mattress stuffing and the fat that comes down the grooves in the bottom of the ovens will be shipped back for soap production. Some have had their skin removed like deer hide. The ashes are spread on the farm fields as fertilizer. Good old German efficiency!

45

SUFFER THE CHILDREN

"Sometimes there are angels masquerading as people"

I don't know the reasoning behind it, but when a child was born dead at Auschwitz, the mother's life was temporarily spared. The dead infant was thrown in the oven. If the child lived at birth, then both mother and child would be sent to the ovens together. Many a mother sacrificed her child when she caught on as to what was happening.

As I mentioned before, Dr. Mengele would take the twins from the parents for experiments. He would do his experiments on one of the twins and the other would be the "control." This child would live as long as the other remained healthy and didn't die from disease or torture. Should the sick one die, then the healthy one would be murdered so that he could perform comparative autopsies on them.

> "Not only Jews, but also gypsies, were the victims of Mengele's perversion of medical sciences. A survivor, Vera Alexander, recalled in the courtroom (after the war) how gypsy twins, one a hunchback, had been sewn together and their veins connected by Mengele who concentrated on blood transfusions in many experiments. 'Their wounds were infected', she said, 'and they were screaming in pain.'
>
> —(The Holocaust pg.689)

More than 1,500 Jewish twins were experimented on by Mengele in the 18 months after his arrival at Auschwitz-Birkenau in May of 1943. Less than 200 survived."

—(The Holocaust pg.687)

The SS weren't known for their patience. It is normal for a child to be hungry and cranky after a long train ride particularly under the circumstances that I have previously told you about. The children were often separated from the parents on the way to the gas chambers. To speed up the process for their quota, bypassing the gas chamber, the SS would merely pick the young children up by their legs, swing these small bodies into a brick wall causing severe trauma to the heads. Then the children would be tossed directly into the furnace. The really sadistic troopers just tossed the irritable, whining youngsters in alive to get their thrill listening to the piercing screams.

46

BEAUTIFUL COUNTRY UGLY MEMORIES

Getting back to the trip that I took to Europe, we also toured Germany quite thoroughly. City after city, town after town, was still in ruins in 1958. The Allied bombing raids had accomplished their goal. The Germans had nothing and were struggling to survive and sensing we were Americans, only made matters worse. It's a beautiful country with ugly memories.

The cruise down the Rhine, in the beautiful wine country, helped you to forget what had transpired there. Every so many miles were the ruins of castles where feudal lords lived and collected passage fees on the river.

To anyone trying to deny that the Holocaust happened, take a stop at any of the major concentration camp sites. Some have maintained a museum-like atmosphere where you can view photographs of buildings with inmates next to them or inside of them crowded on their bunks. You can go inside the buildings if you desire. Bergen-Belsen, where we stopped, had a display of teeth with gold fillings that the SS had apparently overlooked when they ran. Also left, were the tall piles of clothing, shoes, prayer shawls, and eyeglasses in the sorting room.

The most gruesome were the articles made from human skin—lamp shades, covers for books, wallets and clutch purses, etc. The seamstresses were given larger portions of better quality food for creating these sick souvenirs. Pieces made with the exposed tattooed numbers on them were highly prized!

It added to the humiliation to have your name removed and be assigned a number, to be anonymous, and to be devoid of rights and character for the duration of your short life.

> Speaking of numbers, Bruno Brodniewitsch, a German criminal, was assigned the very first number. Number 2 through 30 were common criminals who became the first kapos (SS appointed foremen of labor squads). Numbers 31 through 758 were assigned to the first transport of 728 prisoners. Altogether 4,042,222 official numbers were issued, of which 2,707,261 were assigned to men while 1,334,961 went to women.
>
> —(Cympm.com 11/17/04)

The die was cast, large numbers were already anticipated. Everyone, including children but excluding those selected for extermination, received a number upon arrival at Auschwitz. The numbers were tattooed on the left forearm. Estimates of those not tattooed are two and a half million. (Hans Vanderwerff)

"It is true that tattooed prisoners were murdered and their skin tanned. I myself saw this happen to 200 prisoners…who were executed because of their tattoos. In order to preserve the freshness of their tattoos, the executioners made haste to remove the skin before the body turned cold."

"It was the wife of an SS officer who popularized this method. Every tattooed prisoner was brought to her. If she found his tattoo to her taste, the prisoner would be killed and the skin removed. Then the skin would be tanned and made into mementos (lamp shades, wall hangings, book bindings, etc.)." (Inside The Concentration Camps pg. 106)

47

FIRST HAND KNOWLEDGE

I can further attest to the fact that this Holocaust happened as business competitors of mine, Ernst and Ida Guthmann were spared death but were tattooed, as I saw their arms myself. We were on our way to an advertising trade show in Dallas and my ticket was for a seat next to them.

It was a small world as their son, Stephen, went to the same school and lived in the same neighborhood, as I did. He never once mentioned to me what his parents experienced but I sure got an education on that plane ride. It's hard to believe the horrible. It is so horrible that our minds won't process the information as plausible.

Walt and Anna Kozlowski were really nice people to have as next-door neighbors. He was a hard-working welder and she was a homemaker raising their children. When we first moved into the neighborhood, Walt would wander over to see what I was doing in the garage. I was always building something or other and he, being handy with tools, wanted to see if he could be of assistance. When I think about it now, he probably was just lonesome.

He always relished kidding me about what he called my "Irish garden." The fact that I grew potatoes or used up good garden space to grow them amused him. We were constantly comparing the size of tomatoes and zucchini squash as to who had the "greenest" thumb.

Anna loved to come over to see Mackenzie and Chelsea with her grandchildren. We had a backyard swing, sandbox, and pet rabbits to keep them occupied.

One particular day, later in the morning, I heard something out front near our porch. When I got to the door, Walt was standing there crying (this was to happen several more times). I went out to see what was troubling him. My first thought was that he had injured himself with a power tool. We sat on the porch for a few minutes until he composed himself, to the point where I could understand him.

He had fallen asleep on the couch at his house and apparently had a reoccurring nightmare about his past. He was grabbed by the Germans when he was only 16 years old and was pressed into forced labor for the next 5 years. He came into close contact with the Jews on several occasions and would try and warn them to run into the woods. Those Jews brought in from other parts of Europe, probably didn't understand his warnings in Polish. He saw what the Germans were doing to the prisoners, firsthand.

When the war had ended and he was living over here in Central New York, there was a church function that he and his first wife went to. A discussion came up with the parish priest about eating meat on Friday, which then was considered a sin. The priest told him that he would go to hell if he ate meat upon which Walt fired back that he hadn't had meat over that 5 year period and that now he'd eat meat whenever he felt like it! He went on to explain to the priest that these church laws didn't faze him because, you see, he had already been to hell! A parishioner was lost that day by the priest's insensitivity. He didn't go to church any more.

He then told me the truth about potatoes—that's what he had to eat just about every day for five years and now he couldn't stand to look at them.

I'm getting nightmares just from my research. I can't imagine having lived through that period of time as an eyewitness.

Walt was strong but his first wife couldn't cope with her experiences over there. She committed suicide a few years after arrival here.

I visited Anna a few weeks ago to obtain more information, to fill in the blanks. She told me that Walt was born in 1923 in Northern Poland and that she was born in Frankfort, Germany in 1928. She too had been married before. She told me that the last place Walt worked for the Germans was in a town called Michelstadt. She wasn't sure of the spelling. He was moved from place-to-place because of his carpentry skills.

In their family room is a picture of Anna, her mom and dad, and her two brothers. One lives here, the other in Germany. Her dad is pictured in a regular German Army uniform—not SA or SS. He was home on leave and would never return again. He had worked building the fortifications in France that were supposed to keep the Allies at bay. His last assignment was in Yugoslavia where his unit (similar to our sea-bees) was attacked by the partisans and wiped out.

Before leaving to go back to duty, he asked his family to pay attention to his words. He related to them what monsters the SS were. He said that the atrocities they would later hear about were true. They, the Germans, had done such things that the world would hate them for, forever! I thought it was interesting that Walt had room in his heart for forgiveness to marry a German girl after all that he had been through.

Elsie Ertinger was my secretary for many, many years retiring in 1978. I had known her for over 40 years.

There was a severe depression in Germany after WW I and she told me that they could readily see from the anti-Semitic slogans on the walls of buildings in later years, what was coming under Hitler's regime. The economy was so bad, she told me, that the women would come to the place of employment of the husband to get their paycheck on Friday, take it directly to the bank as the value would drastically drop the next day. Her relatives that stayed were afraid of the SS and were warned not to talk about what was going on for fear of reprisal.

Her family fled from Metterzimmern near Bietigheim, Germany as so many intellectuals did. She arrived at Ellis Island in 1925 at the age of 12. Her brother, Gustave, (they called him Gus) ended up being a bombardier for the U.S. Army-Air Corps. She told me that he pressed the button releasing bombs on his own home town knowing that relatives were still living there. She visited Germany as often as she could after the war to keep in touch with survivors. She brought back an illegal Nazi coin for me, with a swastika on it, knowing that I had a coin collection. It's probably very valuable today.

I received a letter from her son the other day in response to some questions I had for him about prejudice against the Germans living here. Richard wrote to me:

> "There was some prejudice before, during and after WWII. I was born in 1944 and my mom and dad intentionally didn't teach me to speak German so I wouldn't get harassed by the other kids in the neighborhood. However, the "North Side", where I grew up, on Oak Street, was heavily populated by first and second generation Italian and German immigrant families, so I never felt any prejudice personally. Gus, however, often told of being called a "little Nazi" when he was in middle and high school prior to the war. He graduated from college at the Forestry School at Syracuse University. He was stationed in England during the war and married a girl from Wales."

Richard, her son, goes on to say in another letter that was her eulogy,

"There is a quotation I've always liked. I've seen it attributed to the great American author Samuel Clemens, who we know as Mark Twain, but I've never been able to verify that. The quote goes something like this, 'We make a living by what we take...but we make a life by what we give.' When I think about my Mom, I see a person who was a giver all her life. I believe a person's character is strongly shaped by the circumstances and events of their lives. Consider leaving Germany as a twelve year old girl with her mother and younger siblings, with the post war (WWI) economy there in shambles, arriving off the boat in New York City with thousands of other similar immigrants, being processed through Ellis Island like a commodity, not a person, finding your way from the docks to the train station, and then arriving in Syracuse sometime past midnight. Later that very next morning as she was being led by the hand to the nearest public school...no one spoke any English."

Elsie and I had a nice long visit one day at the nursing home where she lived for awhile. She was 92 years old and was still as sharp as a tack! I treated her to real German food that I brought with me, for her lunch. Hospitals and nursing facilities just don't fix ethnic foods. She was in a wheelchair and shared a room with another lady. She was probably as unhappy there as my mom had been in her facility.

She went to the Lord on May 25, 2005 and will be thought of most often for her smile that started each day of work. She was a perfectionist so I don't know who worked for whom. Nothing replaces that old work ethic that seems to have vanished today.

"With My Last Breath, Let Me See Jerusalem" was written by the survivor, Leo Neuman. Mr. Neuman ended up living and working here in Syracuse as a tailor. I had placed a call the other day to his home and left a message that I would love to sit down over a cup of coffee and chat about his experiences in his book. His son returned my call and mentioned that his dad passed away on Thursday, March 17th. I was just six days too late. Perhaps his son will meet me some day for coffee. I'd like that. The book is very well written and I'd enjoy discussing it with him.

The Preface to Eugene Aroneanu's book, *"Inside the Concentration Camps,"* sums it up better than I can say:

"These eyewitness accounts of life and death in the Nazi concentration camps of the Third Reich are shocking, touching, moving, and unforgettable. They are stories of unbelievable horror, unbearable suffering, and incredible courage. Millions perished under circumstances of unimaginable degradation, their voices silenced, seemingly forever.

Fortunately, the war ended before the Nazis could finish their hellish job, and thousands of prisoners survived to tell us their own stories as well as the stories of those whose lives had been so cruelly and so casually terminated.

These accounts chronicle, in grisly detail, unspeakable crimes against helpless, innocent people. What is important to remember is that they are true stories told by people who were there and saw with their own eyes the atrocities that were committed hourly against anybody the Nazis did not like. If you were too old, too young, too fat, too thin, you could be disposed of.

They enjoyed punishing one person for another person's 'crimes' or slaughtering hundreds of hostages on the slightest pretext. Ultimately, in an act of diabolical irony, they could kill you simply because you had seen too much and could testify to what you saw. After all, the last thing they wanted to leave behind was an eyewitness.

Fortunately, many eyewitnesses did survive. And fortunately Eugene Aroneanu was passionate enough about Nazi crimes against humanity to conduct interviews and record the accounts of 100 of these survivors who had been interned in camps throughout Germany and German-occupied territory.

The greater the crime, the harder it is to believe. This tendency toward self-deception can be found in all who took Hitler's teachings to heart. Even now they act as if they doubt the crimes the Nazis committed, preferring rather to ignore them. In so doing, they implicate themselves in the crimes.

If noble-minded Germans want to build a new Germany, how can they know how this Germany should be created if they have no idea what to replace the old with? How will the Germans of tomorrow be able to fulfill their duties properly if the Germans of today ignore the legacy of yesterday's Germany, namely the crimes of the Third Reich?"

—(Eugene Aroneau, 1946 Inside The Concentration Camps-Introduction)

48

I.G. FARBEN at AUSCHWITZ—MONOWITZ—BUNA

"**Bayer** gives me a headache"

I mentioned earlier in the book that I would address KL Auschwitz-Monowitz or sometimes called KL Auschwitz-Buna separately. This facility, Auschwitz III was located just east of Oswiecim. At this location was a conglomerate of businesses called Internationale Gesellschaft Farbenindustrie Aktiengesellschaft or I.G. Farben AG, for short. The AG distinction refers to a German stock corporation. They now have a hybrid KGaA which is Kommandit Gesellschaft auf Aktien which you might see after company names. There are organizations with GmbH and OHG as well. I do have considerable information on I.G. Farben AG which I'll share with you in quoted articles (not my words).

I talk about I.G. Farben at Auschwitz III on its own because it is still with us today! I don't want a hardened heart, but the information on this company and its divisions, troubles me to no end! Again, I stress, these are not my words:

ABCNEWS.com by Brian Ross
Terre Haute, Ind., June 11

Headaches for Bayer—Auschwitz Survivor Says Pharmaceutical Giant Aided Nazis. Holocaust survivor Eva Kor is determined to find out who was behind the medical experiments to which she was subjected in Auschwitz during World War II. (ABCNEWS.com)

"For many in this town, it comes as no surprise that a 65-year-old real estate agent by the name of Eva Kor would be taking on one of the world's biggest companies over something that happened decades ago during World War II. In fact, she's often been accused of over-reacting when the subject has come up. 'Nobody really understood why I reacted the way I reacted and why I could not ignore it,' says Kor.

Orphaned in Auschwitz

This is why: Kor was one of 180 children liberated from the Auschwitz concentration camp at the end of the war. Her parents were killed. And at the age of 10 she and her twin sister Miriam became the subjects of painful, mysterious medical experiments by the notorious Nazi Dr. Joseph Mengele.

'The supervisors would get very nervous and say, 'Mengele is coming!' she recalls. 'And we'd straighten out like little soldiers, because everybody was scared [afraid] of him.'

Mengele especially valued twin children for his experiments. He castrated, blinded and beheaded them; he infected them with disease.

Years after the war, Eva and Miriam suffered serious health problems. Eva never stopped wondering whether there was a connection with Mengele's experiments, involving what she says were hundreds of injections of unknown substances from unknown sources.

'They would tie down my arm with a rubber hose, both arms. They took a lot of blood from my left arm, and they gave many injections in my right,' she says. 'We didn't know. They were not marked. Nor were they volunteering any information.'

Archives Suggest Bayer-Nazi Link

But now, some 55 years after the fact, Kor thinks she may be about to solve the mystery. Going through a recently published book that chronicles Nazi documents from the Auschwitz archives, she made a startling corporate connection.

In a summary of a letter from a doctor working for the huge German pharmaceutical company **Bayer**, she read about **Bayer** experimental drugs to be tested on Auschwitz prisoners. If true, it means that Kor and others were essentially used as laboratory animals.

Bayer is one of the best known and largest pharmaceutical and chemical companies in the world. But what's turning up in these long-forgotten archives puts the company in a much different light.

For example: One of the SS doctors at Auschwitz, Dr. Helmut Vetter, a longtime **Bayer** employee, was involved in the testing of **Bayer** experimental vaccines and medicines on inmates. He was later executed for giving inmates fatal injections. 'I have thrown myself into my work wholeheartedly,' he wrote to his bosses at **Bayer** headquarters. 'Especially as I have the opportunity to test our new preparations, I feel like I am in paradise.'

Victims Seek Restitution

Kor was shocked by what she found. 'For a big company like **Bayer** to be involved in such evil, perpetrated on small children, or innocent people for no other reason than to make money,' she says, 'it's very difficult to accept.'

Now Kor is the lead plaintiff in a class-action lawsuit brought against **Bayer** in Federal Court in Terre Haute, claiming **Bayer**, with the help of Mengele and the Nazis, injected healthy inmates with toxic chemicals and germs to intentionally make them sick in order to test its experimental medicines.

The people who run **Bayer** today were not the people who ran **Bayer** then—a fact that Kor acknowledges but dismisses: 'They have benefited; they should pay restitution.... The corporation is the same corporation.'

But that's very much in dispute in Leverkusen, Germany, where **Bayer** has been headquartered since the 1890s. Its executive offices are now decked out as a giant aspirin box to celebrate the 100th anniversary of its best-known product.

Bayer Says It's a Different Company

No one at **Bayer** headquarters would agree to be interviewed on the record for our report. In fact, **Bayer** took the highly unusual step of banning *20/20* from its annual news conference, citing the questions we might ask.

Instead, a **Bayer** spokesman simply restated the company's official response to the lawsuit—that **Bayer** is not responsible because during the war it was simply a subsidiary of a larger company, I.G. Farben, which now only exists on paper.

'Today's **Bayer AG** is neither identical to, nor is **Bayer** the successor to I.G. Farben,' said Bayer representative Thomas Reinert. 'There is no doubt about the evil that happened.'

Asked repeatedly whether **Bayer** experimental drugs were tested on inmates at Auschwitz, Reinert refused to comment, saying only, 'Bayer did not exist as a legal entity between 1925 and 1951.'

Kor's lawyers disagree. 'Oh, they were there,' says attorney Mel Weiss. 'And they're trying to use a fiction to pretend they weren't.' Weiss says that by accepted legal standards, the **Bayer** Company of today is, in fact, the **Bayer** of World War II. 'We follow the money,' Weiss says. 'We traced the assets. We traced the personnel. And when you put it all together, it's the same.'

Weiss has become hugely successful by bringing controversial class-action lawsuits against some of the biggest corporations in America. Now he's using some tactics, without charging his usual fee, on behalf of victims of the Holocaust.

New Evidence May Show Responsibility

Bayer says the matter was settled years ago at the Nuremberg war crimes trial, when three executives of its then-parent I.G. Farben were acquitted after prosecutors failed to prove the company knew of what was happening at the camps.

But the Nuremberg judges did not have a number of documents only recently discovered, including a letter in which one of the men acquitted—**Bayer** Sales Director Wilhelm Mann—praised Mengele's experiments and promised to discuss financing from the company. 'I have enclosed the first check,' Mann wrote. 'Dr. Mengele's experiments should, as we both agreed, be pursued. Heil Hitler!' **Bayer** says there's no evidence any money was actually sent.

'If this document is true,' says Professor Wolfgang Eckart, director of the Institute of Historical Medicine at Heidelberg University, 'there is a very clear link between what Mengele did and who did his financial support.'

Because of postwar treaties, it's only been in the last few years that German companies could be sued for what happened at places like Auschwitz. And when we came to Auschwitz we were shown things that had never been seen publicly. Most telling: In a locked storeroom, on a stack of dusty shelves, the prominent **Bayer** trademark on an original box of experimental drugs—Number Be 1034, according to the archives, an experimental medicine for typhus.

According to Eckart, typhus matches what Kor has described she went through in the Auschwitz medical labs. 'I was given five injections,' says Kor.' That evening I developed extremely high fever. I was trembling. My arms and legs were swollen, huge size.'

Survivors Show Resolve

And Kor says Mengele was personally involved. 'Mengele and Dr. Konig and three other doctors came in the next morning. They looked at my fever chart, and Dr. Mengele said, laughingly, 'Too bad, she's so young. She has only two weeks to live.'

Hundreds of twins did die from such experiments. Eva and her sister Miriam survived, but as adults Eva suffered from miscarriages and tuberculosis. Her son had cancer. Miriam's kidneys never fully developed and she died of cancer.

'I want to know why my sister died,' Eva Kor says. 'I want to know why all the other twins died.' The answers to her questions may lie in the **Bayer** archives from the war years, located in a building deep inside the **Bayer** compound. But neither Kor nor *20/20* was allowed to see the files—even as **Bayer** maintains it has done nothing wrong and has no connection to what happened during the war.

'It says to me that they're still hiding the ball,' says Weiss. 'And that's what we're going to use American courts for.'

Kor is convinced: 'They were involved,' she says. 'They were in Auschwitz; we know that for a fact. They have prepared the injections that we were injected with. What were those injections? Fifty-five years later, I would like to know.'

Bayer Reacts to Allegations

Bayer continues to contend that it was a different company during the dark days of Nazi Germany, that it was simply a subsidiary of a larger company.

There are a number of German firms other than **Bayer** that have come under fire for alleged experimentation on concentration-camp inmates. Just last month, two other companies were named along with **Bayer** in yet another lawsuit.

And just Thursday, **Bayer** was among more than a dozen companies and banks that announced plans to set up a billion-dollar-plus fund to benefit Holocaust victims."

—(Headaches for Bayer www.candles-museum.com/Bayer.htm12/8/04)

My question would be, "Why the money if they're truly innocent?" Their slogan off their own web-site is: *"Bayer: Science for a Better Life"*. I don't think Eva Kor or other Mengele survivors would agree that their slogan is appropriate.

This from another source, quoted verbatim:

Corporate Crime in the Pharmaceutical Industry During World War II and its aftermath:

"The collective evil of many pharmaceutical companies is manifest even though so many 'nice people' work for them. Hoechst and **Bayer**, the largest and third largest companies in world pharmaceutical sales respectively (in

1984 and before mega-mergers of the 90s), are descended from Germany's I.G. Farben company. Farben ranks with the Standard Oil Trust as one of the two greatest cartels in world history. After the Second World War, the Allies broke up I.G. into effectively three companies: **Hoechst, BASF,** and **Bayer**.

Twelve top I.G. Farben executives were sentenced to terms of imprisonment for slavery and mistreatment offences at the Nuremberg war crimes trials. I.G. built and operated a massive chemical plant at Auschwitz with slave labour; the I.G. facilities at Auschwitz were so enormous that they used more electricity than the entire city of Berlin.

Approximately 300,000 concentration camp workers passed through I.G. Auschwitz. At least 25,000 of them were worked to death (Borkin, 1978:127). Others died in I.G.'s drug testing program.

The following passage in a letter from the company to the camp in Auschwitz, demonstrates the attitude of I.G. Farben to the subjects of its drug testing program:

> 'In contemplation of experiments with the new soporific drug, we would appreciate your procuring for us a number of women.... We received your answer but consider the price of 200 marks a woman, excessive. We propose to pay not more than 170 marks a head. If agreeable, we will take possession of the women. We need approximately 150...Received the order of 150 women. Despite their emaciated condition, they were found satisfactory.
>
> We shall keep you posted on developments concerning this experiment...The tests were made. All subjects died. We shall contact you shortly on the subject of a new load' (Glover, 1977: 58)

Borkin (1978)* has documented in horrifying detail how today's leaders in the international pharmaceutical industry brutalized its slave labor force in their quest to build an industrial empire to match Hitler's political empire.

After the war, the Allies insisted that none of the convicted war criminals be appointed to the boards of the new I.G. companies.

Once Allied control loosened, however, Hoechst in June 1955 appointed Friedrich Jaehne, one of the twelve war criminals sentenced to imprisonment in Nuremberg, to its supervisory board. In September of that year he was elected Chairman.

Bayer appointed Fitz ter Meer, sentenced to seven years at Nuremberg, as Chairman of its board in 1956."

(*Borkin, Joseph 1978, The Crime and Punishment of I.G. Farben, Free Press, New York.)
(Corporate Crime in the Pharmaceutical Industry-The origins of Bayer AG www.healthwatcher.net/Bayer/bayercrimes.html12/8/04)

Should you research: Press Release from the 50th anniversary of the Nuremberg trials on 27 October 96—Demands on **Bayer**—Notes and further Information on multinational chemical companies issue 2/95. Published by the Coordination gegen BAYER-GEFAHREN e.V./CBG Postfach 15 04 18—40081 Dusseldorf titled: *Bayer predecessor financed torture in concentration camps*. I quote verbatim:

> "The 50th anniversary of the inauguration of the Nuremberg Trial on October 27th put the **Bayer** Company in the public spotlight. **Bayer** played a decisive role in human experiments with deadly outcomes during the Third Reich.
> The Allied powers conducted the process against the Nazi doctors who committed torture only half-heartedly because they were interested in their research results. That is why so many of them came to hold high positions in the Federal Republic of Germany and in the USA after the war. The people behind unspeakable countless suffering committed in the name of science were also never brought to justice. The I.G. Farben and **Bayer** companies were never punished for financing Auschwitz's terrifying Josef Mengele or for delivering Cyclone (Zyklon) B from Uerdingen.
>
> *The Responsibility of I.G. Farben*
>
> I.G. Farben is the union of **Agfa, BASF, Bayer, Hoechst**, and a few other smaller German chemical companies. At that time, they had a leading role as the world's biggest chemical company. With amounts of 81 million Reich Marks, they were the biggest single financier of the Nazi party from 1933 to 1944. They explicitly conducted their own plans for the war. They had Hitler's personal assurance guaranteeing delivery of fuel, ammunition, etc., which gave the Nazis the possibility to start the war.
> They in turn won 6 million Reich Marks. I.G. Farben, with branches and connections all over the world, made earnings on both sides of the front. Nazi and Allied bombers were fueled with I.G. Farben petrol. The cartel earned their money from deadly weapons, the industrialization of the mass murders in concentration camps, the massive enslavement of prisoners and 'enemies of the people' as well as from 'the transfer of enemy assets out of conquered areas'.

I.G. Farben maintained contact with the SS through the so-called 'Friendship circle for the leaders of the SS.' Approximately thirty representatives from German companies were members of this circle. I.G. Farben was represented by board member, Butefisch. Prisoners were bought by the SS for the trifle amount of RM (Reich Mark) 170.

They were then subjected to brutal torture sometimes while conscious and sometimes they were already dead. This was done under the pretext of 'medical and scientific experiments in the service of science'.

The mass murders of Jewish people were 'perfected' with the poisonous gas Cyclone (Zyklon). B. I.G. Farben built a new factory near the Auschwitz concentration camp to take advantage of cheap labor. Two million dollars was provided for the construction of the concentration camp.

At I.G. Farben's own Auschwitz, I.G. Monowitz, and the adjacent factory, approximately 370,000 prisoners died as a result of the working conditions and malnutrition. I.G. Farben Board Member, Schneider, displayed the following principle in 1943, 'get out as much work out of the prisoners as possible. All these people should be fed, housed, and treated, so as to get the most work done with the least possible costs.'

Due to this sort of treatment, the average life expectancy at the I.G. Monowitz factory was only 9 months.

The Bayer Control Center

The control center for I.G. Farben conducted human experiments (that) came from **Bayer**. The notorious scientific department was directed by Wilhelm Mann. He was also manager and a member of governing board of the Cyclone (Zyklon) B monopoly, Degesch. He carried out the annihilation of Jews with indifference and recognized human experimentation as an example of progress.

The **Bayer** researcher, Prof. Gerhard Domagk, conducted human experiments for germ warfare under contracts from the SS. He was later awarded the Nobel Prize for medicine for his discovery of sulphonamide. Sulphonamide was first tested on humans who were infested with gangrene and finally treated with antibiotics from Bayer. Death was inclusive. (www.mega.nu:8080/ampp/bayer.html12/8/04)

Factories that had previously made fertilizer now made high explosives. Scientists who in peacetime had worked on pharmaceuticals and dyes, now turned their hand to poison gas...(Jeffreys pgs. 118–119)

Eva said recently: "Emotionally I have forgiven the Nazis, but forgiveness does not absolve any perpetrator from taking responsibility for their actions. I am free. I refuse to forever be a prisoner of Auschwitz. I am free. But they are not and they never will be until they accept their responsibility. They are different people today. I know that the ones who ran **Bayer** fifty years ago are all dead now. But the company today should have the courage and decency to admit their past." (Jeffreys 191–192)

>Other suggested reading on **Bayer**:
>www.bayer.com/about_bayer/history/1925_1945/page1210.htm11/19/04
>www.clublet.com/c/c/why?page=IGFarben12/8/04
>www.stockmaven.com/cobooksA3.htm2/3/05
>www.candles-museum.com/Bayer.htm
>www.candles-museum.com/bayer_acknowledgement.htm
>www.hannibal.net/stories/021999/SurvivingMengele.html12/8/04
>www.cannabisculture.com/forums/showthreaded.

php?Cat=&Number=816301&page=&view=&sb=5&o12/8/04
>www.google.com/

search?num=30&hl=en&lr=&q=Jenny+Miller+%22Bayer+buys+Berkeley12/8/04
>BAYER BUYS BERKELEY by Jenny Miller in Z Magazine January 1998
ASPIRIN by Diarmuid Jeffreys

All of this is giving me a headache. I think I need a **TYLENOL**.

49

HENRY "HEINRICH" FORD

I attended a six part series titled, *"History of the Syracuse Jewish Community"* this past winter at Temple Adath Yeshrin. The program was hosted and moderated by Rabbi Sherman. As I remember, it was the third night in the series that the Rabbi was talking about Jews of notoriety connected to Syracuse and the name Louis Marshall was mentioned. In the course of the conversation, Henry Ford, the automaker, was somehow involved with Mr. Marshall. There also appeared to be an "inside joke" about **Ford** products and the lack of Jewish customers which, at the outset, I didn't know the connection.

Ford grew up in an era of economic stress where the railroad scandals and the economic depression following the Civil War were blamed on the bankers, and the assumption was they were all Jews. He was growing up in a period when the term, "Rothchild" meant an international banker. A typical ranting of the time which he probably was subjected to over and over went like this:

> Wherever on the globe commerce exists,
> There hovers the hooked-nosed Jew with his bag of gold,
> Carrying the curse of usury,
> Like the money changers of old. (Baldwin pg. 29)

"Prejudice does not depend upon actual experience for its power. Anti-Semitism does not require the presence of Jews, only their images…" (Baldwin pg.30)

"There has always been a correlation between economic frustration and actual or symbolic pogroms which tend to remain latent in more ordinary times. Jews are historically disliked most actively in periods of economic depression, when a sense of disenfranchisement and frustration can give rise to illusions of unfair persecution. This, in turn, can lead to an exaggerated self image of 'goodness' that has been abused, causing the unsophisticated 'naïve Christian' to turn with expedient antipathy toward the Jews as the reason for his hardship." (Baldwin pg.30)

Ford viewed the Jews as "ghost people," those nomadic individuals without a country that he felt did not contribute to society but instead were,"takers." He felt that farmers contributed and others lived off them in one way or another. He further felt that he and the Jews didn't have the same value system. They were the Wall Street vultures circling above waiting for Ford to ask for a loan of "eastern cash."

Ford's factory was in Dearborn, Michigan and this is where he started his own newspaper called the *Dearborn Independent*. He hired editors that shared the same hatred and anti-Semitic feelings that he harbored over 90+ issues that went out to rural America under the title," *The International Jew—The World's Problem."* Questioned at one point why it was titled, "International", his response was, "Well, you can't single them out. You have to go after them all. They are all part of the same system." (Baldwin pg.103)

"This nation—his headquarters known as Zion—will bring together all Jews, congenitally 'linked in a fellowship of blood' with each other. The fear of Jewish unity is traced back to the Middle Ages.... The latest example of this influence was vividly seen in stricken Germany.

If you were in Hitler's office in Munich, you could read the German version of, *'Der International Jude: einWeltproblem: Das erste amerikanische Buch uber die Judenfrage, herausgegeben von Heinrich Ford.'* If you went from the waiting room to the inner office you would view a large, framed portrait of Henry Ford above Hitler's desk.

From across the sea, someone was listening to Henry Ford's rhetoric. "We look to Heinrich Ford as the leader of the growing Fascist movement in America." (Baldwin pg.185)

Ford was invited and encouraged by the Germans to establish a manufacturing plant in Germany. Ford Motor Company AG was established in Berlin-Plotzensee and four years later a second factory in Cologne, Ford-Werke AG.

**As many as 1,000 trucks per month were produced in Germany for the Nazis as well as passenger cars for the Wehrmacht, the SS, and the police.

More than 60% of the three-ton, tracked trucks were made by Ford-Werke AG for the German army. This German division also made vehicles for Japan.**

The production was accomplished by forced labor groups behind barbed-wire under Nazi supervision. (Baldwin pgs. 312–315)
Somehow I'm not surprised at any of this. It all seems so logical now.
"With ninety-five cents in his pocket, nineteen-year-old Jacob Marshall arrived in New York City from Germany. The year was 1849. He went to work for the railroads and wended his way upstate, settling in Syracuse. Six years later, established in the hide and leather business, Jacob married Zilli Strauss." (Baldwin pg.116)
Louis was the first of six children by Jacob and Zilli. He had a busy time growing up attending school then working in the family business when he came home. By the time he graduated from high school, he could speak French, German, Latin, Greek, Hebrew, and, of course, English.
He went on to Columbia to study law and did his apprenticeship in Syracuse with Nathaniel B. Smith. So bright and challenged was he that he took one year of studies in the morning while taking the second year in the afternoon. He attended Temple Concord, the oldest in Syracuse, while working on voter's rights and the New York State constitutional convention. He eventually was off to New York to join the law firm of Samuel Untermyer where he joined Temple Emanu-El and later became its president.
He argued the landmark case of *Leo Frank vs. The Sheriff of Fulton County, Georgia.* The young Jew was convicted of murder in Atlanta, and lynched. From that time on he fought against discrimination of Jews in the workplace, the schools, the professions, the armed forces, clubs, hotels, YMCAs and immigration restrictions. He then took on Henry Ford by himself directly, but that would be a book in itself. Your local library should carry information for your edification. It's very uplifting.
The Louis Marshall Memorial Hall is situated on the Syracuse University campus and, ironically, it was in this building that I studied history while attending S.U.

50

WRAP UP

"First and Third Armies were advancing in mostly rural areas, untouched by the war. The GIs were spending their nights in houses. They would give the inhabitants five minutes or so to clear out. The German families were indignant. The GIs were insistent. As Lt. Max Lale put it in a March 30th letter home, 'none of us have any sympathy for them, because we all have been taught to accept the consequences of our actions—these people apparently feel they are the victims of something they had no hand in planning, and they seem to feel they are being mistreated."

—Stephen E. Ambrose-Citizen Soldiers (Our Finest Hour-pg.167)

On television the other day, the History Channel was doing a broadcast about the First Army, particularly the U.S. 3rd Armored Division. This unit, led by General Maurice Rose were the very first to enter Germany—not to be confused with the Third Army led by Patton. Rose entered German soil before Patton. Patton took the credit.

"General Rose, known as 'Spearhead' to his men because he was always out front, was leading his men toward a key city called Paderborn. ...'looming out of the darkness came a huge enemy tank. There was no turning back. Colonel Brown and Shaunce clipped the second of the lumbering vehicles but managed to slip through. The third Panther swiveled sideways in the road. Colonel Brown shot through the narrowing gap, hit the tank and tore the front fender off his jeep (peep). Shaunce, desperately attempting the impossible, came to a jarring halt, pinned by the mass of German armor on one side and a tree on the other. A German tanker shouted a stream of guttural commands and leveled a machine pistol.

It was impossible to tell what exactly happened next. General Rose, Major Bellinger, and T/5 Shaunce stood before the Nazi tank. There was a fog of unreality about the whole situation. The enemy soldier was undoubtedly frightened, and probably trigger-happy. Perhaps he thought that General Rose was attempting to reach for a pistol.

It was dark there on the narrow road. Clouds obscured the moon. Shaunce saw the enemy tank commander as a dim silhouette. He saw the man unaccountably scream a final word, swing the burp gun and fire! There was an agonizing moment when the ripping sound of the weapon, the spout of flame and the sight of General Rose falling forward were all fused together like a nightmare. And then Shaunce yelled and ran. So did Bellinger. General Rose had moved his hand to drop his weapon but the German shot him in the head.' (Another Jew was murdered!)

It was in this way that the great commander of the 'Spearhead' Division came to his death. His military decorations include the Distinguished Service Cross, Distinguished Service Medal, Silver Star with two oak leaf clusters, the Legion of Merit with an oak leaf cluster, the Bronze Star Medal with an oak leaf cluster, Purple Heart with an oak leaf cluster, French Legion of Honor, French Croix de Guerre with palm and the Belgian Croix de Guerre with palm." (www.3ad.org/wwii_maurice/rose)

As I write this part of the book on January 25, 2005, there are 2 days until the 60th anniversary of the liberation of Auschwitz at 2:30 p.m. when the Russians entered the gate to set some 7,650 prisoners free—free to do what?

Some 10,000 liberated were to die in the next 2 weeks as their bodies could not process the food that they were given. Their internal organs had long shut down. Those that could walk in their weak state, found no comfort when they finally returned home. Their homes and businesses had been seized and had been given to others. They had been given up for dead—no one wanted them around. The only clothes that they had were the striped uniforms they were wearing—no money—no food—no family—no place to worship, but they were free!

"I pray you to believe what I have said.... I have reported what I saw and heard, but only part of it. For most of it I have no words."

—(Edward R. Murrow radio broadcast on 4/15/45)

More than 60 years have passed since the end of WW II, and many of those who could speak or write of it have been lost to us forever. For every story not told, the world is poorer. (Our Finest Hour-pg.192)

"Millions of wise, intelligent Jews, whose brilliant minds could cope with any situation, paid with their lives for believing the greatest lie in humanity's annals. The only thing that can be said in their favor is that the truth was so preposterous, so impossible, that even history, which doesn't record many new things under the sun, had no precedent in all its texts for a deed of this magnitude."(Bau-pg.75)

In "Fiddler on the Roof", Tevye says to Lazar Wolf, "Maybe that's why we always wear our hats." The comment is in regard to the fact that over the centuries, the Jews for generations have been forced off their land. The Russians have given them 3 days to vacate their land. Lazar Wolf responds, "Maybe we should give an eye for an eye, a tooth for a tooth" to which Tevye replies, "Then we'd all be blind and toothless."

I was watching the movie TOBRUK the other night, and if I remember the scene correctly, the actor, George Peppard is commenting on how the Jews have been kicked around for some 2,000 years, or more, and he says that he's going to Israel after the war where: "Anyone looking for trouble in the future, will know where to find us!"

As a verse in the song goes, "I have said all that I could, between the evil and the good."

"Preaching against hatred is like being on a treadmill—you feel good doing it, but you get nowhere."(Jack Edgerton-2005)

My book is now finished and from my initial thought process, up to this paragraph, more than two years has gone by. I have learned a great deal not only about events outside of my realm, but more importantly, about myself. True emotions came forth and at times were very cathartic and confessional.

Yesterday was Palm Sunday and I was thinking after dinner, sitting by the fire with my coffee, how lucky we are in this country of ours to be able to express our religious feelings without the persecution that was in Europe some 60 years ago and longer.

Chelsea, our daughter, was in the Passion play at St. Ann's in Manlius. And then later in the day I went to see my grand-daughters, Natalie and Laurin, at the Purim Festival at the Jewish Community Center in Dewitt. I thought of all those young, Catholic, Jewish, Gypsy, and Jehovah's Witness children that are not here today and I ask, why? WHY? What did they, and their parents do, to deserve that kind of termination to their precious lives? Please reach out to others that carry this hatred to this day. The venom they spew is from anger within, prompted by ignorance and intolerance.

Hitler was real and his actions were real. There is no denying that he ranks with Stalin, Pol Pot, Tojo, Amin, Hussien, Suharto, and Mao as a master of genocide. We need to be ever vigilant that this NEVER happens again.

Just yesterday, a young neo-Nazi follower shot and killed 9 people and wounded 7 others before taking his own life on a Chippewa Native American reservation. One of the victims was his own grand-father!

The Greater Syracuse Jewish Community-Wide Holocaust Remembrance

The program lists the following Shoah survivors from the Syracuse area:

Mrs. Lily Benveniste—Bergen Belsen

Mrs. Dora Davis—Auschwitz-Birkenau, Bergen Belsen

Mr. Nathan Davis—Auschwitz-Birkenau, Bergen Belsen

Mrs. Miriam Levinson—Germany 1938 escapee

Mr. Joseph Elman—Puuzana Ghetto

Mr. Max Fishman—Wierznik, Auschwitz

Mrs. Max Fishman—Auschwitz, Bergen Belsen

Ben Schine—Auschwitz, Dachau, Bergen Belsen, Buchenwald

Mrs. Inge Grundel—Lodz Ghetto, Czestochova

Mr. Herbert Grundel—Auschwitz

Mr. Rudy Grundel—Bremen Labor Camp

Mrs. Edith Grundel—Stutthof, Neustadt

Mrs. Toby Kalman—Auschwitz-Birkenau

Mrs. Sarah Slomovic—Auschwitz, Bruntal

—"From Liberation to the Pursuit of Justice" Program.

APPENDIX for 1943

JANUARY

George Washington Carver died in Tuskegee, Alabama. He was born a slave in Missouri in 1861. He earned his masters degree in agriculture from Iowa State and developed new uses for soy beans, sweet potatoes, peanuts, and other crops.

German Field Marshal Paulus surrenders the German 6th Army to the Russians at Stalingrad. Paulus disobeys Hitler's orders to fight to the last man. The city was encircled by the Russians with no supplies or food coming in. The Germans lost 90,000 to starvation and another 100,000 were killed in the last 3 weeks.

Churchill, DeGaulle, and Roosevelt meet in Casablanca.

The Japanese retreat from Guadalcanal.

The Pentagon Building in Washington, D.C. is completed at a cost of $83,000,000. It is the largest office building at the time—6 ½ million square feet.

The German Luftwaffe starts raids on London, England

The American 8th Army captures Tripoli in North Africa.

Nazis mobilize women for the first time.

FEBRUARY

Written on February 1, 1943 by FDR to Mr. and Mrs. T.F. Sullivan

Dear Mr. and Mrs. Sullivan,

The knowledge that your five gallant sons are missing in action against the enemy inspires me to write you this personal message. I realize full well there is little I can say to assuage your grief.

As Commander-in-Chief of the Army and Navy, I want you to know that the entire nation shares in your sorrow. I offer you the gratitude of our country. We who remain to carry on the fight will maintain a courageous spirit, in the knowledge that such sacrifice is not in vain.

The Navy Department has informed me of the expressed desire of your sons, George Thomas, Francis Henry, Joseph Eugene, Madison Abel, and Albert Leo, to serve in the same ship. I am sure that we all take heart in the knowledge that they fought side by side. As one of your sons wrote, "We will make a team together that can't be beat." It is in this spirit which in the end must triumph.

I send you my deepest sympathy in your hour of trial and pray that in Almighty God you will find the comfort and help that only He can bring.

Very sincerely yours,
Franklin D. Roosevelt
(Our Finest Hour—page 152)

The USS Juneau was hit and sunk by the Japanese in the Solomon Islands. Aboard were the 5 Sullivan brothers who wanted to serve together, but died together. The only remaining child was Genevieve who was a Wave in the U.S. Navy.

Hard liquor is banned in the U.S. Army by the War Department.

Rationing starts for oils, fats, butter, coffee, sugar, and gasoline leading to the slogan "use it up, wear it out, and make it do, or do without."

The Russians recapture Kursk.

Franklin Delano Roosevelt orders a 48 hour work week in war plants.

U.S. 8th Army reaches Tunisia.

U.S. Marines add a women's unit headed by R.C. Streeter as the first woman Marine Corps Major.

Americans are buying all the canned goods they can carry as rationing will start 3/1 on processed food. Leather becomes scarce and shoes are also rationed.

MARCH

Field Marshal Rommel (The Desert Fox) returns to Europe from Africa defeated, ill, and exhausted.

Germans close the Krakow Ghetto and start to liquidate all the Jews living within.

The Russians are forced from Kharkov by the Germans.

Montgomery (British) breaks through the Mareth Line in North Africa.

APRIL

Warsaw Ghetto uprising begins, the Germans liquidate 70,000 inhabitants, SS chief Jurgen Stroop proclaims, "The Jewish quarter of Warsaw is no more".

The meat and cheese rationing starts.

U.S. forces land in the Aleutian Islands.

The Germans surrender in Tunisia.

The Jefferson Memorial in Washington is dedicated.

Ruhr dams in Germany are bombed by the British RAF.

We have 2 more years to wait for Hitler to commit suicide (4/30/45)

War essential workers are prohibited from leaving their jobs.

MAY

The Warsaw Ghetto resistance collapses—no Jews are left—very few escape. SS chief, Jurgen Stroop estimates 56,065 are dead.

JUNE

Heinrich Himmler orders the complete liquidation of all ghettos in Poland and Russia—Bedzin, Lvov, Bialystok, Czestochowa, Tarnow, Minsk, Vilna, and Riga.

Goebbels announces that Berlin is now free of all Jews.

Coal strikes start in the U.S. affecting some 60,000 workers.

There is rioting in Detroit, Michigan. African-American leaders say rioting is inspired by the American Nazi Party. (info.detnews.com/history/story/index.cfm)

Income Tax withholding starts.

U.S. Supreme Court rules that children no longer have to salute the flag in schools.

JULY

Mass graves are discovered near Winniza.

Allied troops invade Sicily with the aid of 3,000 war ships and transports. They quickly take Palermo.

Mussolini resigns and is arrested. He is replaced by Marshall Badoglio per order of King Victor Emmanuel.

At the Battle of Kursk, 1,000 larger German tanks are out-maneuvered by much faster Russian tanks. Flame throwers are used to disable the German tanks through their ventilation systems.

Germans are now in retreat on all fronts.

"The Big Inch" (oil pipeline from Texas to Pennsylvania) is dedicated.

AUGUST

600 Jews escape in uprising at Treblinka, Poland

John F. Kennedy's boat, PT-109 is sunk

U.S. troops take Messina, Sicily

Russians retake Kharkov

SEPTEMBER

We have 2 more years to wait for Japan to surrender (9/2/45).

The Allies land in Italy and the Italian government secretly surrenders to General Eisenhower.

When the surrender is finally announced, Mussolini, assisted by the Nazis, escapes by plane to Germany.

The Russians capture Smolensk—The U.S. 5th Army captures Naples.

The U.S. Merchant Marine Academy is dedicated at Kings Point, NY.

Victory ships go into production.

The ship, Brennan, is the very first ship to be transported overland across the Rocky Mts.

OCTOBER

The rescue of Jews begins in Denmark.

300 Jews escape from Sobibor concentration camp.

Italy declares war on Germany

The Chicago Subway opens.

NOVEMBER

U.S. troops invade the Solomon Islands

The U.S. Army seizes control of the American railroads.

U.S. coal miners end their 6 month strike for a $1.50 per day increase.

The Russians capture Kiev.

Churchill, Roosevelt, and Stalin meet at Tehran.

Marshall Tito (Joseph Broz) becomes the leader of the Yugoslavia government. Tito has been friendly to the Allied cause and is very popular with his countrymen.

The first all female fire department is formed in Ashville, NY.

FDR and Churchill meet with Chinese leader Chiang Kai-shek and his wife in Cairo, Egypt. She serves as the interpreter since he speaks very little English. This meeting recognizes China as a major power as they discuss plans to defeat the Japanese and move their influence out of the South Pacific and Manchuria.

DECEMBER

The German battleship, Scharnhorst, is sunk off the coast of Norway by the British.

General Eisenhower is named Supreme Commander of Allied Forces for the upcoming invasion of Europe.

There are 9 major train wrecks in 1943 but in my research I can't find where anyone feels that a sabotage issue involving the American Nazi Party should be explored: 5/23 Delair, NJ, 7/6 High Bluff, TN, 8/4 Stockton, GA, 8/29 Wayland, NY, 9/6 Frankfort Jct., PA, 9/14 Dewey, IN, 12/16 Buie, NC, 12/27 Almont, Ont., and 12/31 Bagley, VT.

IN GENERAL:

Harvard goes co-ed.

Jacques Cousteau and Emile Gagnon develop the aqua lung.

Bergen-Belsen concentration camp is erected.

Irish coffee is served for the first time to shivering passengers on trans-Atlantic flying boat flights.

The balance of power begins to shift in favor of the Allies due to better convoy methods and improved air coverage resulting in safer crossings. Added to this is the better detection of U-boats, longer range of planes, and code-breaking procedures.

Allies begin the island hopping campaign towards Japan.

3,323,970 entered military service through the Selective Service System.

150,000 prisoners in U.S. prisons and jails produce over $100,000,000 worth of war goods.

The government is paying $18.75 per ton for scrap metal.

I want to acknowledge and "thank" the following sources and individuals for the information that I obtained to make this project as accurate and complete as possible. Their writings and research were most valuable. This research at times was most difficult, very thought provoking, and a definite learning experience. The nightmares will subside, someday.

BIBLIOGRAPHY

LIBRARY SOURCES:

Aroneanu, Eugene. Inside the Concentration Camps Translated by Thomas Whissen. Praeger Publishing 1996

Bailey, Ronald H. The Home Front Time-Life Books 1977

Baldwin, Neil. Henry Ford and the Jews-The Mass Production of Hate Public Affairs 2001

Bau, Joseph. Dear God, Have You Ever Gone Hungry? Arcade Publishing 1998

Bernstein, Carl and Politi, Marco. His Holiness-John Paul II-The Hidden History. Doubleday 1996

Brockett, Oscar G. History of the Theatre. Boston, Allyn, Bacon 1968

Bronner, Edwin J. Encyclopedia of American Theatre. A.S. Barnes 1980

Daniel, Clifton. Chronicle of the Twentieth Century. Chronicle Publishing 1987

Ford, Gerald. The Twentieth Century. Hamlyn Publishing Group Ltd. 1989

Grun. The Timetables of History Simon and Schuster 1979

Hilliard, Robert L. Ph.D. Surviving the Americans. Seven Stories Press 1997

Jeffreys, Diarmuid. ASPIRIN. Bloomsbury 2004

Kane, Joseph. Famous First Facts. H.W. Wilson 1981

Karolak, Tadeusz. John Paul II-The Pope from Poland Interpress Publishing Warsaw 1979

Korbonski, Stefan Jews and Poles in World War II

Landau, Ronnie S. The Nazi Holocaust. Ivan R. Dee 1992

Lucas, Dr. Richard C. The Forgotten Holocaust

Millgate, Linda. The Almanac of Dates. Harcourt Brace Jovanovich 1977

National Geographic. Eye Witness to the Twentieth Century. National Geographic Society 1998

Neuman, Leo With My Last Breath, Let Me See Jerusalem. Sacred Heart University 1999

Rees, Laurence. Auschwitz. BBC Books 2005

Rhodes, Richard. Masters of Death. Alfred A. Knopf 2002

Toland, John. Adolf Hitler. Doubleday 1976

Weigel, George. Witness to Hope-biography of John Paul II. Cliff Street Books 1999

Articles:

Moorman, James W. When Martin Luther King Was Killed The Associated Press The Post Standard 6/14/05 Senate Apologizes For Failure to Stop Lynchings

INTERNET SOURCES:

www.virtualmuseum.com/exhibitions/orphans/English

www.Holocaust.com Simon Wiesenthal center

www.USHMM.org United States Holocaust Memorial Museum

www.History.ACUSD.edu gen/WW2 Timeline/Camps Nazi Concentration Camps 1933–1945

www.jewishvirtuallibrary.orgsource/holocaust/cc.html American-Israeli Cooperative Enterprise List of Major Companies Involved in the Death Camps: I.G. Farben, Bayer AG, BMW, Daimler-Benz, Krupp, Agfa, BASF, Messerschmitt, Shell, Siemens, Volkswagen, Zeiss-Ikon, Zeppelin,

www.holocaustforgotten.com/journey.html11/15/05

www.soulofamerica.com/cityfldr2chicago15.html12/22/04

www.news.bbc.co.ukAmerica'sDayOfTerrorTIMELINE1/6/05

www.geocities.com/Heartland/Acres?4711/AdolfHitler.html12/21/04

www.pbs.org/wgbh/pages/frontline/shows/pope/etc/synopsis.html

www.satinballroom.com/features/USO.html/

www.cghs.dade.k12.us/holocaust/heydrich.html1/19/05

www.holocaustforgotten.com/non-jewishvictims.htm11/15/04

www.holocaustforgotten.com/African.htm11/15/04

www.holocaustforgotten.com/poland.htm11/15/04

www.info.detnews.com/history/story/index.cfm?id=185&category=events11/10/04

www.en.wikipedia.org/wiki/1943_in_music11/10/04

www.en.wikipedia.org/wiki/1943_in_film11/10/04

www.en.wikipedia.org/wiki/1943_in_aviation11/10/04

www.en.wikipedia.org/wiki/1943_in_science11/10/04

www.en.wikipedia.org/wiki/1943_in_sports11/10/04

www.en.wikipedia.org/wiki/1943_in_literature11/10/04

www.en.wikipedia.org/wiki/1943_in_television11/10/04

www.en.wikipedia.org/wiki/List_of_state_leaders_in_194311/10/04

www.amazon.com/exec/obidos/tg/detail/-/158648303X/qid=1105633203/sr=1-1/ref...1/13/05

www.amazon.com/exec/obidos/tg/detail/-/0465085717/qid=1105633055/sr=1-23/ref...1/13/05

www.history1900s.about.com/library/holocaust/blauschwitz.htm11/12/04

www.secondworldwar.co.uk/ahitler.html1/22/05

www.secondworldwar.co.uk/casualty.html1/22/05

www.guardian.co.uk/germany/article/0,2763,1391937,00.html1/21/05

www.guardian.co.uk/germany/article/0,2763,1386676,00.html1/21/05

www.guardian.co.uk/germany/article/0,2763,1393659,00.html1/21/05

www.guardian.co.uk/germany/article/0,2763,1391956,00.html1/21/05

www.commondreams.org/views03/1006-08.htm1/21/05

www.veritas3.holocaust-history.org/questions/hitler-jewish.shtml1/12/05

www.pbs.org/auschwitz/learning/timeline/1/20/05

www.um.oswiecim.pl/anniversary/1/14/05

www.um.oswiecim.pl/pl/index.php?newlang=english1/14/05

BIBLIOGRAPHY 187

www.um.oswiecim.pl/a.../index.php?option=com..
content&task=view&id=31&itemid=41/14/05

www.um.oswiecim.pl/a.../index.php?option=com..
content&task=view&id=41&itemid=51/14/05

www.pbs.org/auschwitz/learning/timeline/1943.html1/20/05

www.nizkor.org/hweb/people/h/hitler-adolf/oss-papers/text/oss-profile-05-02.html

www.nizkor.org/ftp.cgi/camps/auschwitz/cyanide/cyanide.0012/14/05

www.pbs.org/auschwitz/40-45/background/1/20/05

www.pbs.org/auschwitz/40-45/victims/1/20/05

www.pbs.org/auschwitz/40-45/killing/1/20/05

www.pbs.org/auschwitz/40-45/liberation/1/20/05

www.pbs.org/auschwitz/40-45/murder/1/20/05

www.pbs.org/auschwitz/40-45/corruption/1/20/05

www.pbs.org/auschwitz/40-45/factories/1/20/05

www.pbs.org/auschwitz/40-45/orders/1/20/05

www.pbs.org/auschwitz/40-45/beginnings/1/20/05

www.pbs.org/auschwitz/40-45/index.html1/20/05

www.worldatwar.net/biography/p/petain/1/27/05

www.rotten.com/library/bio/nazi/adolf-hitler/1/22/05

www.3ad.org/wwii..heroes/rose..maurice..home.htm2/9/05

www.myherald.com/viewstory.cgi?paperid=1&sid=sh222002&q=Homestead-South12/1/03

www.google.com/ search?num=30&hl=en&lr=&q=Jenny+Miller+%22Bayer=buys=Berkeley 12/8/04

www.healthwatcher.net/Bayer/bayercrimes.html 12/8/04

www.clublet.com/c/cwhy?page=IGFarben 12/8/04

www.candles-museum.com/Bayer.htm 12/8/04

www.mega.nu:8080/ampp/bayer.html 12/8/04

www.bayer.com/ 11/19/04

www.bayer.de/page18.htm 11/19/04

www.bayer.com/about_bayer/history/1925_1945/page1210.htm 11/19/04

www.fcit.coedu.usf.edu/holocaust/maps/AusLg.htm 11/12/04

www.cympm.com/auschwitz.html 11/17/04

www.jewishvirtuallibrary.org/jsource/Holocaust/auenvironmap.html 11/17/04

www.mazal.org/Maps/Auschwitz-01.htm 11/17/04

www.wsg-hist.uni-linz.ac.at/Auschwitz/HTML/Trans-2.html 11/17/04

www.fcit.coedu.usf.edu/holocaust/MAPS/map008.htm 11/17/04

www.ushmm.org/wlc/printmedia.php?lang=en&FileType=MA&MediaId=362&ArticleTitle... 11/17/04

www.ushmm.org/wlc/article.php?lang=en&ModuleId=10005161 11/17/04

www.ushmm.org/wlc/printmedia.php?lang=en&FileType=MA&MediaId=358&Art... 11/17/04

www.fcit.coedu.usf.edu/holocaust/gallery/jewpop.htm 11/12/04

www.ushmm.org/wlc/article.php?lang=en&ModuleId=10005687 11/17/04 www.fcit.coedu.usf.edu/holocaust/sitemap/sitemap.htm 11/12/04

www.ccju.org./ccju_ccju_publications_breath.htm 12/8/99

www.fcit.coedu.usf.edu/holocaust/GALLFR2/FAUSC17.htm 1/13/05

www.fcit.coedu.usf.edu/holocaust/GALLFR2/FAUSC01.htm 1/13/05

www.fcit.coedu.usf.edu/holocaust/GALLFR2/FAUSC35.htm1/13/05

www.wsbd.net/travel/auschwitz/photo1.html1/13/05

www.zchor.org/lidice1.htm1/19/05

www.actiontales.com/chacko_d/man_comments.html 1/19/05

www.history1900s.about.com/library/holocaust/blmap.htm 11/12/04

www.fcit.coedu.usf.edu/holocaust/resource/gallery/maps.htm11/12/04

www.ms101.mysearch.com/jsp/
GGcres.jsp?id=4NgQqaYM4HMJ&su=http%3A//ms101.m...1/6/05

www.fcit.coedu.usf.edu/holocaust/MAPS/SNDMAP/mapp2.htm11/12/04

www.stockmaven.com/cobooksA3.htm2/3/05

www.ccju.org2/21/05

www.racematters.org/turningawayfromholocaust.htm2/21/05

www.ushmm.org/lectures/kalb.htm2/21/05

www.en.wikipedia.org/wiki/Genocide#Genocide_in_history3/22/05

www.en.wikipedia.org/wiki/Emmett_Till6/16/2005

www.watson.org/-lisa/blackhistory/early-civilrights/emmett.html6/16/2005

www.merck.de/servlet/PB/menu/1404520_ePRJ-MERCK-
EN_pcontent_12/content.h...2006

www.merck.de/servlet/PB/menu/1404520_ePRJ-MERCK-EN_pcontent_12/content.h...4/20/06

DVD Format: "Broadway the American Musical" PBS-Public Broadcasting System
"The Third Reich in Color"
"John Paul II-The Millennial Pope at the Crossroads of History"-Frontline Helen Whitney Productions-PBS

ACKNOWLEDGEMENTS:

Personal: Walter and Anna Kozlowski-Liverpool, NY (Walt-deceased)
Ernst and Ida Guthman-Syracuse, NY (deceased)
Elsie Ertinger-Syracuse, NY (deceased)
Julita Klopocka-Niemiec-Manlius, NY

A big "THANKS" to Pat Infantine, MLS
David D'Ambrosio, MLS
Helen Vecchio, MLS
Carol Johnson, MLS
Margot Baxter, MLS
Helen Chamberlain, PhD

...and the staff at the Manlius Library for their help and encouragement. Without all of you, I'd be pulling my hair out (what's left).
Thanks to the libraries of Cornell, Colgate, Syracuse University, Hamilton and Lemoyne for the loan of resource material.

Legal review: Edwina C. Schleider, Attorney At Law
Meggesto, Crossett, and Valerino, LLP—Syracuse, New York

A Production of:
The General Store, Inc.—a New York corporation (All Rights Reserved)

Suggested readings:

The Roots of Anti-Judaism in the Christian Environment Creating and Nourishing the Signs of a New Dialogue by Rino Fischella

With My Last Breath, Let Me See Jerusalem by Leo Neuman
www.rotten.com/library/bio/nazi/adolf-hitler/
Auschwitz by Laurence Rees
Aspirin by Diarmuid Jeffreys
Henry Ford and the Jews-Mass Production of Hate by Neil Baldwin

ABOUT THE AUTHOR

Jack Edgerton was born in Syracuse, NY and has resided in Central New York for the past 62 years. He graduated from the Manlius Military Academy, Onondaga Community College, and attended Syracuse University. Jack is the proud father of 8 children—4 boys, 4 girls and is a grandfather as well. By occupation, he has been a third generation importer/wholesaler since joining the family business in 1963. Pursuing his interest in writing, this is his first book of many to come.

978-0-595-39355-8
0-595-39355-1

Printed in the United States
55974LVS00004B/232-243